Landscapes of
MADEIRA

a countryside guide

Fourth edition

John and Pat Underwood

SUNFLOWER
BOOKS

Dedicated to
José Fernandes

*who urged us to see more of his island
and so quite changed our lives!*

Fourth edition
copyright © 1994
Sunflower Books
12 Kendrick Mews
London SW7 3HG, UK

First published 1980
Second edition 1983
Third edition 1988

ISBN 1-85691-002-4

Important note to the reader

We have tried to ensure that the descriptions and maps in this book are
error-free at press date. ***Be sure to check page 136 for any STOP PRESS
comments, or write to us for an 'Update' before you travel*** (see inside
back cover). It is very helpful for us to receive your comments (sent in
care of the publishers, please) for the updating of future printings.
    We rely on those who use this book — especially walkers — to take
along a good supply of common sense when they explore. Conditions
change very rapidly on Madeira, and ***storm damage or bulldozing may
make a route unsafe at any time.*** If the route is not as we outline it here,
and your way ahead is not secure, return to the point of departure. ***Never
attempt to complete a tour or walk under hazardous conditions!*** Please
read carefully the notes on pages 35 to 40, the country code on page 128,
and the introductory comments at the beginning of each tour and walk
(regarding road conditions, equipment, grade, distances and time, etc).
Explore *safely*, while at the same time respecting the beauty of the
countryside.

Cover photograph: Crista de Galo, Vinháticos
Photographs by John Underwood
Touring map by Pat Underwood
Walking maps adapted by Pat Underwood from Portuguese military
    maps; see 'Acknowledgements', page 8
Drawings by Katharina Kelly

Printed and bound in Great Britain by Brightsea Press, Exeter

Contents

4   Landscapes of Madeira

❀ Foreword

To visit Madeira — at any time of year — and not walk the island's paths and trails, up to the mountain crests and ever closer to heaven, is to miss seeing and 'feeling' the island in its full majesty. To know Madeira, we have to cross it with the levadas, listening to the hymn of their waters. We have to experience the sacred silence of the summits. Up there, beside the 'Man on Foot', lost in a veritable sea of clouds, the walker establishes that paradisial rapport that man can at times have with nature.

We Madeirans know that the cascade of the waters, the breath of the flowers, the murmur of the trees, the surge of the springs are the life force of our island — making it a true paradise afloat in the Atlantic. Our soil is impregnated with the sweat and the love of generation upon generation of our people who were born and who died here, carrying out their gigantic life's work of transforming the land into terraces reaching from the sea far up the mountainsides. These builders penned a true epic with their souls, an epic which can only be 'read' and understood by those who tread in their footsteps along the mountain paths.

So we welcome with delight publication of this new edition of *Landscapes of Madeira:* this excellent book is the ideal companion for those who wish to have an authentic experience of our island, with its unending panoramas of majesty and poetry. John and Pat Underwood know the deep secrets of Madeira. Over many years of walking they have penetrated the island as few others have, and they have brought their understanding to the publication of this work. This indispensable guide will help everyone who uses it to discover the enchantments of our land. Our deep thanks and best wishes to John and Pat for their contribution to the tourism of Madeira — an island that welcomes you with the warmth and brotherhood of its people and the exuberance and friendship of its landscapes.

JOÃO CARLOS ABREU
Secretary of Culture and Tourism

✹ Preface

Since we first published a small book of Madeira walks in 1980, not only has *Landscapes of Madeira* become the most widely-used guide to the island, but it inspired a whole series of 'Landscapes' books, which we publish under our Sunflower imprint.

The aim of the series is to give tourists what João Carlos Abreu, in his Foreword, calls 'an authentic experience of the island'. Each *Landscapes* guide is written by someone who knows the terrain intimately and who hopes to lead the visitor off the beaten track and into the countryside — whether by car, public transport, or on foot.

This Fourth edition of *Landscapes of Madeira* features many new walks which, in conjunction with the new walking maps, allow you to devise routes that cover the length and breadth of the island. To supplement and complement this information, we also publish *The Madeira Book*, which is described on page 8 under 'Recommended reading'.

All the Sunflower authors hope to convey more than mere enthusiasm for their chosen landscapes — love might be a better word. Our love affair with Madeira really came into blossom with our 'discovery' of the levadas. They have never ceased to fascinate or inspire us. No matter how tired we may be, to walk beside a levada always refreshes our spirits and brings the bounce back into our steps.

The levadas

Whether you use this book to tour, walk or picnic, we will lead you along the levadas. Such watercourses are not unique to Madeira: what *is* unique is their **accessibility** and **extent.** You need only venture a little way off the main roads to begin to appreciate Madeira's myriad aqueducts — for their beauty, ingenuity of design, and for the courage and determination needed to bring the concept to its present glory. The island's irrigation system now comprises an impressive 2150km (1350 miles) of channels, including 40km (25 miles) of tunnels — and the work started centuries ago.

The earliest settlers on Madeira began cultivating the lower slopes in the south of the island, cutting out terraces (*poios*). Working with contractors (who sometimes used slave or convict labour), they built the first small levadas, which carried water from springs higher up the mountainsides to irrigate their lands. The first legislation dealing with levadas and water rights dates back to the second half of the fifteenth century.

By the early 1900s, there were about 200 of these levadas, meandering over about 1000km (620 miles). Many were privately owned, and the undisciplined appropriation of water meant that the island's most valuable asset was often unfairly distributed. In fact, by the mid-1930s, only two-thirds of the island's arable land was under cultivation — and just half of that was irrigated. Only the State had the money to implement a major building programme and the authority to enforce a more equitable system of distribution.

For there was plenty of water for irrigation, and torrents to spare for power. Clouds driven to the island by the prevailing northeast winds are caught by the central mountain chain, and as much as 2m (80 inches) of rain may fall in the north in a year, while the south coast may be dry for up to six months. In effect the island is a huge self-regulating reservoir, holding up to 200 million cubic metres (45,000 million gallons) of water. The rain seeps down into porous volcanic ash, soon meeting layers of basaltic clay and laterite — both quite impervious. Here the water wells up again in springs and, if not channelled, pours untapped, as it has for centuries, down countless ravines into the sea.

In 1939 the Portuguese government sent a mission to the island to study a combined irrigation/hydroelectric scheme. The 'new' levadas created from its plans are channelled out at an altitude of about 1000m/3300ft, where the concentration of rainfall, dew and springs is greatest. The water is conveyed first to power stations lying just at the outer edge of the arable land (about

600m/2000ft), then it flows down to the irrigated zones. Here, distribution is carried out by the *levadeiro,* who diverts the flow to each proprietor.

Most of the mission's development plans were implemented by 1970. Among the most important projects were the Levada do Norte and the Levada dos Tornos, both of which you will discover as you tour, walk or picnic. Their incredible length, considering the terrain, is best gauged on the fold-out touring map. The work took only 25 years to complete, although it was all done by hand. How were the tunnels cut through the solid basalt? How did the workers channel out the levadas beneath the icy waterfalls, halfway between earth and sky? Often, as during the construction of the corniche road between São Vicente and Porto Moniz, they were suspended from above in wicker baskets, while they fought the unyielding stone with picks. Many lost their lives to bring water and electricity to the islanders … and unending joy to those who 'listen to the hymn of their waters'.

Acknowledgements
We are very grateful for the invaluable help of the following people:
For guiding: Luis de Sousa and John Blandy.
For help with maps and plans: the Regional Government of Madeira, especially Eng Leandro Câmara, Eng Jorge Jardim Fernandes and Eng Felipe Ferreira; and the Instituto Geográfico e Cadastral, for permission to adapt their maps.
For checking the walks: It would be impossible to mention all the people who have contributed suggestions for this new edition; we have received many hundreds of letters since the Third edition was published. Please continue to send your comments; they are helpful to everyone who uses the book. Special thanks, however, to Clive Scott, George Watt, Alec Farmer, Oliver St John, Aubrey McKennell, and Thea Whitworth.
For support and encouragement: the Madeira Tourist Office in Funchal, especially João Carlos Abreu, Secretary of Culture and Tourism, and the Portuguese National Tourist Office in London, especially Pilar Pereira.

Recommended reading
The Madeira Book, by John and Pat Underwood (Sunflower Books). The most complete picture of present-day Madeira in print and an ideal companion volume to *Landscapes of Madeira.* Among the subjects described and illustrated with 350 colour photographs are the volcanic nature of the land, terracing and the levadas, island crafts and industries, housing, festivals, gardens and parks, legends, historical figures associated with Madeira, architecture, and island walks.
Madeira: Plants and Flowers, by Luis Franquinho and António da Costa (distributed by Sunflower Books). The most comprehensive guide to the island's flora available, with identification of more than 400 plants; 700 colour photographs.
Madeira and Porto Santo (Berlitz). All the practical information you need in a pocket-size book, updated annually.

❋ Getting about

There is no doubt that a **hired car** or taxi is the most convenient way of getting round the island — especially for journeys to the north and west. We hope that the liberal cross-references to picnics and walks in the touring section will inspire motorists and walkers to team up on car hire. Note that all the walking maps show the car symbol (🚗) wherever you can park near the path of a walk.

All **taxi** drivers must carry a government-approved price list for journeys outside Funchal. *Don't be afraid to bargain, however.* Your hotel porter may be able to suggest a driver for an all-day tour: some are especially knowledgeable about island culture and customs; a few are keen walkers, too!

Coach tours are the most popular way of 'seeing Madeira in a day'. They provide a painless introduction to road conditions and a remarkable overview of island scenery. You'll discover in comfort the landscapes you'll want to explore at leisure, on your own.

Our favourite way of getting about is by **bus**. The system is economical, reliable, and fun! You get splendid views perched up on bus seats, and most of the buses are new and quite comfortable. The drivers are expert; we always feel safe in their hands. The map on the following pages shows you where to board your bus in Funchal. For 'country' buses, buy your ticket on the bus. For orange 'town' buses, it pays to buy a 7-day tourist pass: see notes at the bottom of page 133. (By the way, don't be confused by identical bus numbers, eg orange town bus 20 to Monte; green/cream country bus 20 to Santo da Serra.)

Please do not rely *solely* on the bus timetables printed in this book (pages 129-133); *changes are frequent.* The Tourist Office sells a **bus timetable** at a nominal charge, but even this is not always up to date. It's best to visit the bus kiosks at the 'bus station' on the Avenida do Mar and amend the timetables in this book according to the latest posted schedules. *It always pays to verify bus departures and seat availability* for long journeys; this can also be done at the kiosks. ***Do** arrive well before departure time.* In Funchal's 'sea' of buses, it may take you several minutes to find the one you want. In our experience, buses leave exactly on time — or a minute or two early.

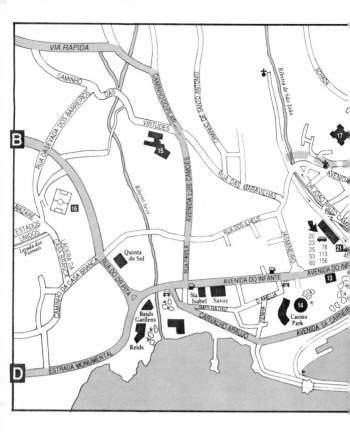

LEGEND

1. Tourist Office
2. Statue of Zarco
3. Blandy Agency and British Consulate
4. Air Portugal (TAP)
5. Municipal Theatre
6. Casa do Turista
7. Government Offices
8. Sé (Cathedral)
9. Old Customs House
10. Infante Fountains
11. Statue of Henry the Navigator
12. Santa Caterina Chapel
13. Quinta Vigia (President's House)
14. Casino
15. Hospital
16. Barreiros Stadium
17. Forte do Pico
18. Quinta das Cruzes
19. Santa Clara Convent
20. Municipal Museum
21. Post Office and SAM Bus Station
22. São Lourenço Palace
23. Colegiate Church
24. Madeira Wine Institute
25. Law Courts
26. Town Hall
27. Museum of Sacred Art
28. New Customs House
29. Market
30. Forte de São Tiago
31. Old Town
32. Boat Trips
33. Power Station
34. Praça da Autonomia
35. Rodoeste Bus Station

ORANGE 'TOWN' BUSES
with departure points

1. to Lombada from **33**
3. to Lombada from **33**
6. to the Lido from **33**
8. to Santa Quitéria from **28**
11. to Trapiche from **28**
16. to Santa Quitéria from **28**
20. to Monte from **34**
21. to Monte from **34**
22. to Babosas from **33**
29. to Romeiros from **33**
30. to the Jardim Botânico from **33**
37. to Palheiro Ferreiro from **33**
45. to Barreiros Stadium from **21**

✝ ⛽ 🚕 church, petrol, taxi rank

10

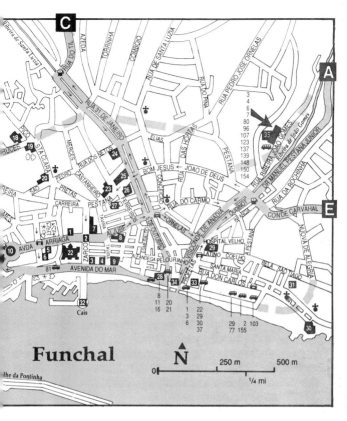

Funchal

N°	Colour/Company	Final Destination	Departure Point
2	red/grey (EA do Caniço)	Assomada	east end of Av. do Mar
3	cream/red (Rodoeste)	Estreito de C.d.L.	Rodoeste bus station 35
4	cream/red (Rodoeste)	Madalena do Mar	Rodoeste bus station 35
6	cream/red (Rodoeste)	Boaventura	Rodoeste bus station 35
7	cream/red (Rodoeste)	Ribeira Brava	Rodoeste bus station 35
20	cream/green (SAM)	Santo da Serra	SAM bus station 21
23	cream/green (SAM)	Machico	SAM bus station 21
25	cream/green (SAM)	Santo da Serra	SAM bus station 21
29	cream/blue (ECA)	Camacha	east end of Av. do Mar
53	cream/green (SAM)	Faial, Igreja	SAM bus station 21
60	cream/green (SAM)	Boqueirão	SAM bus station 21
77	cream/blue (ECA)	Santo da Serra	east end of Av. do Mar
78	cream/green (SAM)	Faial via Machico	SAM bus station 21
80	cream/red (Rodoeste)	Porto Moniz	Rodoeste bus station 35
81	cream/blue (SA Curral)	Curral das Freiras	west side of 22
96	cream/red (Rodoeste)	Corticeiras	Rodoeste bus station 35
103	cream/red (São Roque)	Boaventura	east end of Av. do Mar
107	cream/red (Rodoeste)	Raposeira	Rodoeste bus station 35
113	cream/green (SAM)	Caniçal	SAM bus station 21
123	cream/red (Rodoeste)	Campanário	Rodoeste bus station 35
137	cream/red (Rodoeste)	Estreito de C.d.L.	Rodoeste bus station 35
139	cream/red (Rodoeste)	Porto Moniz	Rodoeste bus station 35
148	cream/red (Rodoeste)	Boa Morte	Rodoeste bus station 35
150	cream/red (Rodoeste)	Porto Moniz	Rodoeste bus station 35
154	cream/red (Rodoeste)	Cabo Girão	Rodoeste bus station 35
155	red/grey (EA do Caniço)	Ponta da Oliveira	east end of Av. do Mar
156	cream/green (SAM)	Maroços	SAM bus station 21

11

✿ Picnicking

In the course of some of our rambles we've come upon easy-to-reach picnic spots that might appeal to those of you who prefer *very* short walks. If you are car touring, they are an 'off-the-beaten-track' alternative to the island's many roadside picnic tables (indicated in the touring notes with the symbol ⧧).

All the information you need to find these more secluded picnic spots is given below, where *picnic numbers correspond to walk numbers*, so that you can quickly find the general location on the island by looking at the touring map (where walks are outlined in white). We give you walking times and transport details. The location of the picnic is indicated by the symbol *P* on the appropriate *walking map*, which also shows the nearest 🚌 stop (if appropriate) and 🚗 parking area.

Please remember to **wear sensible shoes and take a sunhat** (the symbol ○ after the title indicates a picnic **in full sun**). It's a good idea to take along a plastic groundsheet as well, in case it's damp or prickly.

If you are travelling to your picnic by bus, be sure to check our bus timetables (pages 129-133) against the latest schedules shown in the kiosks in Funchal (see 'Getting about', page 9). **If you are travelling by car**, be sure to park *well off* the road; *never* block a road or track.

All picnickers should read the country code on page 128 and go quietly in the countryside.

1 SOCORRIDOS VALLEY (map page 44, photograph page 43)

by car or taxi: 8-10min on foot   *by bus:* 8-10min on foot
🚗 Lombada: Take the northbound road at Vitória (1km east of Câmara de Lobos, signposted 'Pico dos Barcelos/Funchal') to Lombada 0.7km north (Car tour 3).
🚌 1 or 3 to Lombada (orange 'town' bus).
From Lombada, walk northwest up the road and immediately fork right up cobbled 'steps' to climb to the Levada dos Piornais (4min). Turn left; the valley overlook is reached in five minutes. There are two narrow places along the levada (drops of 7m/20ft). **Dramatic valley overlook from a shady eucalyptus grove.**

6 BOA MORTE (map page 54, photographs pages 53, 56)

by car or taxi: up to 25min on foot   *by bus:* up to 35min on foot
🚗 Boa Morte forest: The road is 3km west of Campanário, at the 172km marker — *not* signposted). Continue past Boa Morte to the Levada do Norte, where you can park on one of the tracks (Car tours 1, 5, 6).

12

🚐 127 to Boa Morte (see Short walk 6-3, page 53): Walk up the paved road out of the village to the levada in the forest. Return on 🚐 148.
Turn left on the levada. Picnic anywhere along here, or else follow the levada northwest into the valley of the Ribeira Brava. **There are no views in the forest, but it is an exceptionally lovely setting; continue on the levada to just beyond the concrete viewing platform, for magnificent views of the Ribeira Brava and the Paúl da Serra. Good shade.**

7a PORTO NOVO FROM THE EAST (map page 60, photo page 64)

by car or taxi: 15-20min on foot   by bus: 15-20min on foot
🚗 Levada dos Tornos reservoir: Coming from Funchal on the EN101, take the Gaula turn-off (EN206). After 0.8km fork left. Pass a church on the right 4.3km from the EN101. Some 0.8km north of the church, turn left up a track to a reservoir, easily seen from the road (Car tour 2).
🚐 60 ('Boqueirão' bus): Ask the driver for 'Levada dos Tornos, Lombo Grande'. From the bus stop, walk north up the EN206 for one minute to find the levada crossing.
Turn left on the levada: ten minutes' walking will give you good views, or go as far as the tunnel with 'windows' mentioned on page 65 (20min). **This picnic overlooks the western side of the Porto Novo Valley and is at its best in spring. Some shade nearby.**

7b BOAVENTURA VALLEY (map page 60)

by car or taxi: 30min on foot   by bus: 30min on foot
🚗 and 🚐 as 7a above.
Follow the notes for Short walk 7-4, page 65. **Overlook a golden valley (at its best in summer) and the south coast. Some shade.**

8 PORTO NOVO FROM THE WEST (map page 60, photo page 28)

by car or taxi: 10-15min on foot   by bus: 30-35min on foot
🚗 Assomada, below the levada: Drive up the road on the east side of the church and its parking lot. Bear left *and left again* to pass an electricity sub-station on your left (a squarish grey building, easily seen from the main road). After 1km uphill, you see an old raised water channel on your right. Park here, well tucked in (Car tour 2).
🚐 2, etc to Assomada *church*; then use notes for motorists above.
Follow the path at the left of the raised mill-race up to the levada, then turn right along the watercourse. **You overlook the eastern escarpment of the valley and São Lourenço. Ideal for an early evening picnic.**

10 LEVADA DA SERRA (map page 60, photograph page 27)

by car or taxi: 15min on foot   by bus: 30min on foot
🚗 Levada da Serra: The EN202 crosses the levada 0.5km west of the EN102, between João Frino and Santo da Serra (Car tours 2, 4).
🚐 77 to the Sitio das Quatro Estradas; see Short walk 10-4, page 70.
Turn left and picnic by the levada or below the bridge over the João Frino River. **No far-reaching views, just a lovely setting in spring.**

11 FONTE VERMELHA (map page 79, photograph page 23) ○

by car or taxi: up to 5min on foot   by bus: 5min on foot
🚗 Maroços: The road branches off the EN101-3 (Car tour 2). Park well off the road. By the time this book is in print, the road may be finished to Portela, and you will be able to park near the mill shown on page 23.
🚐 156 to Maroços.
See notes to start Walk 11, page 71. **Idyllic setting by an old mill. Fine basalt formations. No far-reaching views. Little shade.**

12 ABRA BAY (map page 74) ○

only accessible by car or taxi: up to 15min on foot

🚌 Abra Bay: The EN101-3 ends here at a viewpoint (Car tour 2).
Picnic at the viewpoint or the coastal overlook (15min). No shade.

14 PORTELA (map page 79, photograph pages 80-81)

by car or taxi: up to 5min on foot	*by bus: up to 5min on foot*
🚗 Portela, well off the road.	🚌 20, 53 or 78 to Portela.

Follow the road behind the 'Casa da Portela'. It soon becomes a track.
Superb view over Penha de Águia, away from the coaches. Shade.

15 LEVADA DO CASTELEJO (map page 105)

by car or taxi: up to 30min on foot	*by bus: up to 30min on foot*
🚗 Cruz: see 'How to get there', page 81 (Car tour 4).	
🚌 53 to Cruz.	

Follow Walk 15 for up to 30 minutes. **Fine outlook towards Penha de
Águia, or venture into the valley of the Ribeira de São Roque.**

16 PENHA DE ÁGUIA (map page 78, photograph pages 20-21)

by car or taxi: up to 30min on foot	*by bus: up to 30min on foot*
🚗 and 🚌: as Picnic 15.	

*Use the notes on page 83 to follow Walk 16 from the 1h-point part-way
up 'Eagle Rock'.* **Fine views back towards the heights of Portela and the
central mountains. Shade of pines.**

17 POÇO DA NEVE, ARIEIRO (map reverse of touring map)

only accessible by car or taxi: up to 5min on foot

🚗 ice house (Poço da Neve), 2km below Pico do Arieiro (Car tours 1, 4).
Picnic by the ice house (no shade), or below it in the heath tree grove.
Splendid outlook over Arieiro's moorlands and down to Funchal.

18 PICO DO ARIEIRO
(map reverse of touring map, photograph pages 86-87) ○

only accessible by car or taxi: up to 15min on foot

🚗 Pico do Arieiro (Car tours 1, 4).
Picnic near the start of Walk 18 or at the first viewpoint (notes page 87).
Stupendous mountain setting and views. No shade.

19 QUEIMADAS
(map pages 90-91, photographs pages 23, 32, 92)

only accessible by car or taxi: up to 35min on foot

🚗 Queimadas Park (reached by a steep track *west* of Santana) or Pico
das Pedras. See notes for Car tour 4, pages 27 and 28.
*Picnic by the pousada or explore the surrounds (see Short walk 19, page
89).* **No far-reaching views, but a fairytale setting.**

23 ACHADA DO TEIXEIRA (map reverse of touring map) ○

only accessible by car or taxi: 5-50min on foot

🚗 Achada do Teixeira (Car tour 4).
*Picnic at Homem em Pé (the huge basaltic rock on the slopes behind the
house in the parking area; 5min), or follow Short walk 23 (page 99) to
picnic on the Pico Ruivo path or at Pico Ruivo itself (50min).* **Lacks the
drama of Picnic 18, but the settings and views are fabulous.**

25 BALCÕES (map page 105, photograph page 19)

by car or taxi: 20min on foot	*by bus: 20min on foot*

🚗 Ribeiro Frio (Car tours 1, 4).   🚌 103 to Ribeiro Frio.
See notes page 29, first paragraph. **Superb outlook over the central peaks, the Metade Valley and Fajã da Nogueira. Shade nearby.**

26 LAPA DO GALHO (map reverse of touring map, photo p. 109)

by car or taxi: 10-15min on foot   *by bus: 10-15min on foot*
🚗 Encumeada, by the bar/restaurant (Car tours 1, 5, 6).
🚌 6 to Encumeada.
Join the Levada do Norte a few steps up from the road, opposite the bar/restaurant, on the south side of the pass. Lapa do Galho, a fine promontory, is 12min from the road (2-3min before the first tunnel). **Wonderful views to the great peaks; wealth of vegetation on the levada.**

28 BICA DA CANA (map reverse of touring map, photo p. 111) ○

only accessible by car or taxi: up to 10min on foot
🚗 at the entrance (with two stone pillars) to the house (Car tours 5, 6).
Follow the track from the Bica house up to the triangulation point/miradouro (no shade). **Stupendous views of the great peaks. No shade.**

31 RAPOSEIRA (map page 116, photograph page 17)

by car or taxi: 5min on foot   *by bus: 20min on foot*
🚗 Raposeira, at the end of the lane west of the church (Car tour 6).
🚌 107 to Raposeira.
Descend the cobbled lane on the west side of the church until it ends, then continue downhill for a few more minutes on the path. **Fantastic views over the coast and Paúl do Mar. Good shade from pines.**

32 CAMPO GRANDE (map pages 120-121, photograph page 119) ○

only accessible by car or taxi: 5-45min on foot
🚗 by the waterhouse on the EN208, near the statue of Cristo Rei, 9km north of Canhas (Car tours 5, 6).
Use the notes for Walk 32 to picnic anywhere, perhaps by the caves (45min). **Fine views towards the south coast, by a mesmerising ribbon of levada. No shade.**

33a-e RABAÇAL (map pages 120-121, photograph page 123)

only accessible by car or taxi: up to 50min on foot
🚗 Rabaçal, below the Paúl da Serra (Car tours 5, 6). Note: this road is quite vertiginous. You can also get to these picnics by parking on the EN211. See notes for Alternative walk 33-1, page 122. Add another 20 minutes to the walking time, *torch essential.*
There are five picnic choices at Rabacal: (a) 🏠 *by the houses; (b) a suntrap below the houses, at the Rabaçal end of the tunnel (follow Short walk 33-2 down to the Levada das 25 Fontes and turn left); (c) far side of the tunnel, overlooking Calheta's valley (follow (b), then continue past the sun-trap and through the tunnel); (d) the Risco falls (Short walk 33-1); (e) 25 Fontes (Short walk 33-2).* **All of the settings are different, but they all feature watercourses where you can cool your drinks! Some shade.**

35 LEVADA DA CENTRAL DA RIBEIRA DA JANELA (map page 127, photograph page 126)

only accessible by car or taxi: up to 30min on foot
🚗 at the reservoir above Porto Moniz, or in Lamaceiros (Car tour 5). See 'How to get there', page 126.
Use the notes for Walk 35, page 127. **Fantastic views of the great Janela Valley from a very picturesque levada. Good shade.**

 Touring

Driving on Madeira's winding roads can be quite tiring. Don't aim to average more than about 20km/h. Plan leisurely excursions if possible, with walking breaks to stretch your legs. Ideally, we would have described shorter tours, but most people want to get good value from their hired car. **The best one-day excursion is tour 1; tours 4 and 5 make an ideal two-day programme.**

Work is going on all over the island to build new (often EC-funded) **roads**, to the detriment of the older main roads. Although almost all roads are asphalted, *beware of pot-holes and be prepared to meet road-works almost anywhere.* Other **hazards** for motorists are the 'macho' Madeiran drivers, people walking on the roads (perhaps three abreast) because there are no pavements, and cars that stop dead in their tracks, so that the occupants can have a chat.

Our touring notes are brief: they include little history or information that can be found in *The Madeira Book* (see page 8). We concentrate instead on the 'logistics' of touring: times and distances, road conditions, getting to the best viewpoints at the right time of day, etc. Most of all, we emphasise possibilities for **walking** and **picnicking**. If you're picnicking or sharing a car with walkers, you should find the ⌧ symbols on the walking maps useful: these alert you to places where you can park near a walk. And *do* refer to these walking maps from time to time while touring — perhaps when you stop at a viewpoint; they contain a great deal of interesting information.

The large fold-out touring map is designed to be held out opposite the touring notes. City exits correspond to those on the plan on pages 10-11. **Symbols** used in the text are explained in the map legend.

Take along **warm clothing, food** and **drink**; you may experience delays, even on main roads. **Allow ample time for stops**: our times include only short breaks at viewpoints labelled ⌧ in the notes. Calculate time for **detours** as well: places, picnics and walks shown in ( ) are only accessible via detours off the main route.

All motorists should read the country code on page 128 and go quietly in the countryside. *Boa viagem!*

1 MADEIRA NORTH AND SOUTH

Funchal • Ribeira Brava • Encumeada • São Vicente • (Porto Moniz) • Boaventura • Santana • Faial • Ribeiro Frio • Poiso • (Pico do Arieiro) • Monte • Funchal

*129km/80mi; 6-7 hours' driving **without detours** (add 36km/23mi; 2h for the detour to Porto Moniz and 14km/9mi; 45min for the detour to Pico do Arieiro); Exit B from Funchal (plan page10)*

On route: 🚏 at Campanário, Vinháticos, Encumeada, Chão dos Louros, Ponta Delgada, Boaventura, EN103 around Ribeiro Frio, Pico do Arieiro. Picnics (see **P** symbol and pages 12-15): (6), (17-19, 23), 25, 26; Walks 4, (5), 6, (17-22), 23, (24), 25-30

*If you have only one day to tour the island, then this is the circuit to do, **including the detours to Porto Moniz and Pico do Arieiro**. You are in for a very tiring, but very exhilarating day. **Do** leave Funchal **very** early in the morning; we've planned the tour so that you have the best views westwards in the morning and to the east in the afternoon. If, however, you plan to have a car at your disposal for several days, then do Tours 4 and 5 **instead of** this very long expedition — you'll cover all the same routes, with time to spare. Expect to run up against some heavy traffic in the south. In the north, the short stretch of road between Ponta Delgada and Boaventura is very narrow and still cobbled; it is likely that roadworks will be in swing on this stretch. Be warned also: you are very likely to meet tour buses hurtling along the narrow north coast road; you may even be forced to back up quite some distance to let them pass. Occasional pot-holes on almost all roads.*

Head for the Funchal ring road at the statue to Freedom in front of Reids Gardens (Rua do Dr Pita, Exit B). Wherever the new road ends (work will be in progress until 1995/6), continue past **Cabo Girão** (Tour 3), and then **Quinta Grande** (⊕), where you cross the Levada do Norte (Walk 6), and **Campanário** (✗🍴⊕🚏). At the KM172 marker stone, you pass the northbound road to Boa Morte (**P**6) and Fontes (Walk 5), before circling steeply down

The stupendous outlook down over Paúl do Mar, from the pine-shaded viewpoint below Raposeira (Car tour 6, Picnic 31, Walk 31)

São Vicente (Car tours 1 and 5). Part of the village has been lovingly restored, and this is a good place to take a break for morning coffee.

into **Ribeira Brava** (31km ▲▲✕🖳⊕ and ✝ founded in the 1500s). Bright umbrellas cheer the esplanade, where Walks 29 and 30 end.

Leave the village on the EN104 north, along a narrow canyon graced with poplars. After a straight run, the road begins its twisting ascent to **Serra de Água.** You pass two picnic areas (🗺🇦) before reaching the beautifully-situated Pousada dos Vinháticos (41km ▲▲✕🗺🇦), where Walk 27 ends. Walk 4 ends further uphill on the right, by roadworks. Snake up to **Encumeada** (44km ✕; 1004m/3293ft). From this pass there are wonderful views over the north and south coasts. While you are here, *do* take the opportunity to see the great Levada do Norte (*P*26); it's just a minute's walk from the parking area — the steps are opposite the bar/restaurant on the south side of the pass (notes page 107). Walks 26 and 27 begin here on the levada; Walks 28 and 29 begin on the north side of the pass (🗺🇦), where Walk 23 ends (on the opposite side of the road).

Then descend into São Vicente's welcoming valley (🗺🇦), past **Chão dos Louros**, the lovely laurel grove shown opposite (46km WC and 🇦 with fireplaces). Soon you'll have good views (🗺🇦) over Rosário's church and stream: in high summer the hay-ricks weave ribbons of gold into the tapestry of this emerald landscape. Beyond **Rosário** you pass the EN208, under construction to the Paúl da Serra. On your right, on the eastern hillside, there is a graceful clocktower — Nossa Senhora de Fátima.

Come into **São Vicente** (55km ✝✕🖳⊕; photograph above), a good place to take a break for morning coffee … and to make a decision: are you going to try to fit in a detour to Porto Moniz? If it's now later than 10.00, you really don't have the time. If you *do* have time, use the notes for Car tour 5 on page 30 to go at least *part* of the

18

Top: Balcões (Car tours 1, 4; Picnic 25): the Torres have pride of place, with Pico Ruivo to the right; bottom: Chão dos Louros (Car tour 1).

way — to see the waterfalls west of Seixal. This detour is *not* included in our kilometre readings.

On leaving São Vicente, look out for the chapel built into a hollowed-out rock south of the bridge (⛪). Then either turn left towards Seixal or follow the main tour: turn right on the coastal EN101 (🏔✕). After passing through a tunnel, your attention will be drawn to the chequered pattern made by the heath tree hedges protecting the terraces from the fierce northerly winds. Most of the fields are planted with vines, but this is for table wine; the vines which yield the grapes for the fine Madeira wines are generally found in the south, around Estreito de Câmara de Lobos. A narrow cobbled road takes you in shadow below menacing cliffs, before you skirt above the lava-fertile promontory of **Ponta Delgada** (62km ✕🍴) and soar up to a viewpoint (📷🌲) over the village setting and headlands to the east. Almost immediately the road turns inland, leaving the awesome coast for the green-gold gentleness of the great **Boaventura** (⊕🌲) valley. Just past the village (65km) there is a good viewpoint (📷) on the left. At the head of the valley (🍴) a road is being built to Curral das Freiras.

The bucolic pleasures of this valley are a foretaste of the whole unforgettable landscape between Boaventura and Santana. Pass above **Arco de São Jorge** (72km ⊕), decked out with vines and hedgerows and rainbows of flowers. The hillsides are cultivated almost down to the sea, along the sweeping curve (*arco*) of the bay. Climb past mossy cliffs and dark pines brightened by banks of agapanthus, to reach another outlook by a sea-cliff (📷🌲). From here there are excellent views over Arco and back to Ponta

Delgada, where the church and a swimming pool are down by the seashore. Adjacent to this viewpoint is 'Cabanas' (✕). Descend to **São Jorge** (82km ✝♨☕⊕), which boasts the richest baroque church outside Funchal (it is off to the left, below the main road), then pass a road up right to Ilha de São Jorge, where Walk 20 ends. Soon hairpin bends offer enticing views of **Santana** ★ (90km ⛰✕☕⊕), where orchards and market gardens roll down to the sea. If you haven't brought a picnic, this is the best place to stop for lunch.

From Santana the tour travels via the EN101 to **Faial** and then the EN103 to Poiso; use the notes on pages 28 and 29 (Car tour 4). It's about two hours from Santana to Funchal and, hopefully, you will have time to walk to Balcões from **Ribeiro Frio** (Walk 25) and drive to Arieiro from Poiso. Past **Poiso** (115km *excluding* the detour to Arieiro), continue south on the EN103 to **Monte** ★ (123km ✝✿✕). Walk above the delightful gardens to the church of Our Lady of the Mount, where you can see the tiny poignant statue to Madeira's patron saint. From the bottom of the church steps (departure point for the famous toboggan rides), you could follow the agapanthus-banked lane to the left, to Babosas Balcony (ten minutes return on foot). Here a baroque chapel looks out over the impressive bowl of Curral dos Romeiros in the João Gomes River valley. Now it's just 5km back to Funchal.

Terreiros and the peaks, from the viewpoint on Eagle Rock (Car tour 4, Walk 16, Picnic 16)

2 EASTERN MADEIRA'S GENTLE CHARMS

Funchal • Palheiro Gardens • Camacha • Santo da Serra
• Machico • Ponta de São Lourenço • Pico do Facho •
Santa Cruz • Garajau • Funchal

84km/52mi; 4 hours' driving; Exit A from Funchal (plan page 11)

On route: ⊼ on the EN202 north of João Frino, São Lourenço Point, Santa
Cruz, Garajau; Picnics (see **P** symbol and pages 12-15): (7a-b), 8, (10),
(11), 12; Walks 7-13

*A leisurely tour on asphalted, but sometimes pot-holed, roads. Allow all
day — you're sure to want to make long stops at the Palheiro Gardens,
Camacha, and perhaps São Lourenço Point.*

Opening hours

Palheiro Gardens: Monday to Friday (except holidays) from 09.30-
12.30); tickets are sold at the gate.

Leave Funchal on the EN102-1 (Rua Dr Manuel Pestana
Junior, Exit A). Just a few minutes after joining the
EN102 (signposted south to São Gonçalo), you reach the
Palheiro Gardens ★ (5km ✿), on your right. Turn into the
cobbled drive, shaded by planes and lined with lilies and
camellias. Below the house, gentle terraces yield up ever-
changing vistas of the formal and informal gardens, pools
and fountains, avenues and parks surrounding the Count
of Carvahal's original *quinta* and chapel.

From here turn right on the EN102, crossing the Levada
dos Tornos (Walk 7). Now the road runs below the Levada
da Serra (Walk 10), which may be joined at various points.
Continue (✕🍴) up to **Camacha ★** (10km ✕🍴⊕wc), the
centre of Madeira's willowcraft industry. The village
square (the 'Achada da Camacha') overlooks the magnificent Porto Novo Valley. Walk 8 takes you down the

valley (from the 'Centro da Saúde'
here); Walk 7 circles the valley, and
Short walk 7-3 starts here too, at the
right of the Café Relógio.

Passing market gardens, continue to the wooded heights of **Eira
de Fora** (🍴). There is a view down
right over the Levada dos Tornos,
before you come to **Águas Mansas**
(15km) and pass the junction of the
EN206 south (**P**7a-b). Access to
Short walk 10-3 is via the dirt track
on your left, 100m past this turn-off.
Then round a bend to enter the great
basin of the Boaventura River, another valley irrigated by the Tornos.
At 19km pass the EN202 left to

21

Poiso; our favourite stretch of the Levada da Serra begins not far up this road (🚏; *P*10) and takes you to Portela (Short walks 10-4 and 10-5; photograph page 27).

At 21km fork right on the EN207 into **Santo da Serra** (22km ✿✕🚌), a woodland village with several fine *quintas*. Walk 9 starts here; Walk 10 could begin or end here. Beyond the church, ignore the first sharp left turn (just past the park), but bear left at the Y-fork in front of the Quinta da Paz, to skirt the golf course. Bear left again beyond the clubhouse and continue down into Machico's valley (ignore a turning to the right some 0.6km downhill, unless you are taking passengers to Walk 9). Two viewpoints (📷) on this road afford superb perspectives on the flawless setting of emerald-green Machico Bay, Pico do Facho, and the sun-baked arm of São Lourenço.

From the second viewpoint, continue down to the EN101 and bear left for **Machico ★** (30km ⚓🏔✕🚌⊕), Madeira's first settlement. Of particular interest are the Manueline church and the Chapel of Miracles. The latter, on the east side of the river, was founded in 1420 on the site of Zarco's first landfall; destroyed by a flood in 1803, the chapel was rebuilt later in the 19th century.

Make for Caniçal on the EN101-3. Some 100m after joining this road, ignore the branch-off left to Maroços (*P*11; photograph opposite), where Walk 11 begins. You climb the lush eastern flanks of Machico's valley (✕), soon coming to the Caniçal tunnel, where Walk 13 and Short

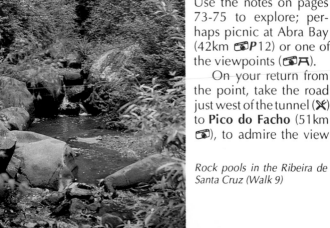

walks 11-1 and 11-2 begin. Unless you wish to visit Caniçal, continue straight out (✕) past the tax-free industrial zone to **São Lourenço Point**. Use the notes on pages 73-75 to explore; perhaps picnic at Abra Bay (42km 📷*P*12) or one of the viewpoints (📷🚏).

On your return from the point, take the road just west of the tunnel (✕) to **Pico do Facho** (51km 📷), to admire the view

Rock pools in the Ribeira de Santa Cruz (Walk 9)

over Machico and its bay, nestling below the hills of Santo da Serra. (Take care turning in the tiny parking area.)

Continuing west, pass **Matur** (🏔🗡) and, just past the turn-off to the airport, bear left into delightful **Santa Cruz** (62km ⛽🏕🗡🛒⊕). Here you can stretch your legs in the *til*-shaded square and visit the bright-white Church of São Salvador, one of the finest Manueline buildings on the island and the largest church outside Funchal.

Bridges soon span the great clefts of the Santa Cruz and Porto Novo valleys. Short walk 8 begins at **Assomada**'s church (*P*8). Just beyond the EN205 up right to Camacha, turn left down to **Caniço** (73km 🏔🗡🛒⊕), a market-garden and tourist centre. Negotiate the one-way circuit, then head right, down a steep cobbled road, to **Garajau Point** (76km ✝🕶🏕). From this sunny promontory, spiked with prickly-pear cactus and 'Pride of Madeira', you have a splendid view of the Deserta Islands and São Lourenço Point to the east and the comings and goings of ships around the Bay of Funchal. The statue here, Christ the King, is a miniature of the famous one in Rio de Janeiro.

From Garajau head up northwest, to **Cançela** (77km 🗡🛒). Don't take the new road here; stay on the narrow EN101-11, hugging the coast. Look out, 2km past Cançela, for a fine promontory on the left (🕶) called 'The Pinnacle', from where the views over Funchal are superb. Beyond **São Gonçalo** (80km 🗡🛒) you will pass another bougainvilla-fringed overlook (🕶) closer to the city.

Top: The old mill at Fonte Vermelha (Walk 11, Picnic 11), near Maroços, is where the Levada do Caniçal takes its source. Notice the fine basalt prisms behind the mill. Bottom: The shady Levada do Caldeirão Verde meanders between Queimadas and Pico das Pedras (Picnic 19 and Short walk 24-1). This is a good place to stretch your legs during Car tour 4.

3 THE CORRAL AND THE CAPE

Funchal • Pico dos Barcelos • Eira do Serrado • Curral das Freiras • Câmara de Lobos • Cabo Girão • Funchal

71km/44mi; 4 hours' driving; Exit B from Funchal (plan page 10)

On route: ⊼ at Cabo Girão; Walks (3), 6. (Picnic 1 and Walks 1 and 2 are near the route of this tour, but are more easily reached direct from Funchal by public transport.)

This tour is suitable for morning or afternoon. The road between Funchal and Cabo Girão is heavily congested and subject to roadworks. The EN107 to Curral das Freiras is not for the faint-hearted driver or nervous passengers: mostly cobbled, it flaunts many hairpin bends and sheer drops past the Eira do Serrado. These precipices are all the more obvious since mid-1992, when forest fires ravaged the entire area. It will be several years before this route regains its beauty.

Leaving Funchal at the statue to Freedom in front of Reids Gardens (Rua do Dr Pita, Exit B), follow signs for Pico dos Barcelos. You approach the church of São Martinho — an island landmark — on a hill. Turn right just before the church, climbing the EN105 to **Pico dos Barcelos** ★ (6km ✕ ✆ WC), an aloe-collared *miradouro* offering fine views of the Funchal setting and the east.

Continue north on the EN105, bearing left after 0.5km, then right (at a minor junction 0.7km further on), and finally left again after another 0.6km. You have joined the EN107 to Curral, and you climb through forests of

Approaching Pico do Cedro (Walk 3). During this tour you could take a detour up to the Jardim da Serra (14km return), to see the quinta shown opposite or do Short walk 3. To get there, take the northbound road out of Estreito (signposted 'Jardim da Serra'). You cross the Levada do Norte (just beyond a shrine on the left; Walk 6 starts here) and then go through Corticeiras (where Walk 3 begins). To begin Short walk 3, park at the Quinta Mis Muchachos (see map page 47).

If you take the detour described in the caption opposite, from Corticeiras continue on the road marked with a dotted green line on the map on page 47. You approach one of the island's most enchanting landscapes, the aptly-named 'Garden of the Mountain Range' (Jardim da Serra). The jewel in this setting is the lovely quinta shown here. It was built in the 1800s by the English consul, Henry Veitch. From here he sent fruit, books and old wines to Napoleon, when the Northumberland laid anchor in Funchal harbour on its passage to St Helena. Unfortunately, the road north of the quinta is now too poor for hired cars.

eucalyptus and pine, splintered by golden sun-shafts. A good viewpoint (📷) over the Socorridos ravine is passed on the left, before you reach the right-hand fork to the **Eira do Serrado** ★ (16km 📷WC). It's a 15-minute (return) walk to this viewpoint, from where there are stupendous views over Curral, 400m/1300ft below.

Beyond the Eira the road becomes increasingly vertiginous (and fire-ravaged), as it circles down into **Curral das Freiras** ★ ('The Nuns' Corral', 20km ✗WC), set below awesome heights. The village is a focal point for many of the island's most challenging walks, but some can no longer be recommended, due to fires, storms … and continuing roadworks. Walk 3 ends down by the river.

Return to São Martinho and pick up the ring road west, then follow signposting to Câmara de Lobos. At the crossroad (✗🍽) into **Câmara de Lobos** ★ (✗⊕ and ✝ founded by Zarco in 1424), notice the terrace on the left. It was from here that Sir Winston Churchill painted the curving white arc of the village against the backdrop of the awesome red cape, Cabo Girão. Returning from the village, bear left uphill for 1km. Then turn off right up to **Pico da Torre** (📷), a fine viewpoint over Câmara de Lobos, before continuing west.

The winding road crosses the Levada do Norte (Walk 6) west of Garachico. Soon reach the left-hand turn to **Cabo Girão** ★ (51km ✗🍴📷WC). Atop this cliff, safe behind iron railings, you can marvel at the toy ships at sea some 580m/1900ft below you … and at the tenacity of the sure-footed Madeiran farmers working their tiny terraces.

Return east on the EN214, past a fork up left to Estreito de Câmara de Lobos (58km ✗⊕). The island's best grapes are grown around here. Return to Funchal on the ring road or via the old road beside the coast, passing the Lido ★.

4 MOUNTAINS AND MORE MOUNTAINS!

Funchal • Terreiro da Luta • Poiso • Pico do Arieiro • Portela • Porto da Cruz • Achada do Teixeira • Santana • (São Jorge • Arco de São Jorge) • Faial • Ribeiro Frio • Funchal

*141km/88mi; 6 hours' driving, **excluding** the detour to Arco de São Jorge; Exit A from Funchal (plan page 11)*

On route: ☐ at Poiso, Pico do Arieiro, EN202 north of João Frino, EN103 around Ribeiro Frio, Pico das Pedras, EN101-5, path from Achada do Teixeira to Pico Ruivo, Queimadas Park; Picnics (see **P** symbol and pages 12-15): 10, 14-19, 23, 25; Walks: 7, 10, 13-18, (19-22), 23-25

It is usual to include the mountainous northeast of the island in what is often called a 'Santana Tour', covering all of central Madeira (our Car tour 1). We find this very hectic and urge you to devote an entire day to visiting the great rugged peaks and the gentle moorland roads radiating from Poiso Pass. This tour fits in nicely with Car tour 5, providing a leisurely two-day introduction to many of Madeira's best landscapes. Start out early in the morning and aim to reach Arieiro no later than 09.30; clouds often descend by about 10.00, obscuring the wonderful view of the peaks. If you do not plan to take any short walks, you will have time to go further west than Santana — to São Jorge (18km return; 40min) or possibly Arco (38km return; 1h30min) — a part of the island not to be missed. Although this tour is long, the roads are all asphalted and good, although winding and occasionally pot-holed.

The direct route to Arieiro from Funchal is Exit C (Rua 31 de Janeiro; EN103), via Monte. But we suggest you try another way: take Exit A and use the notes on page 21 as far as the **Palheiro Gardens ★** (5km). In a minute more, you will encounter the EN201 joining from the left. Turn up left here and follow this pine- and eucalyptus-shaded road northwest (crossing the Levada dos Tornos; Walk 7), to **Terreiro da Luta ★** (14km † ☐WC). Here a statue to Our Lady of Peace commemorates the sufferings of the people of Funchal during World War I. Round the base of the statue there is a rosary made from the anchor chains of ships torpedoed in Funchal harbour. In the early 1900s a luxurious funicular railway climbed up here via Monte. The views over the city's setting are superb, but soon you must *press on!* Join the EN103 ahead and turn right. The smooth asphalt road* lined with hydrangeas and lilies snakes its way up to a barren plateau and finally **Poiso Pass** (1400m/4600ft; 20km ✕☐☐).

Here turn left on the highland road (EN202) to Arieiro. Sheep dart about in the morning mists, munching gorse and bilberry — *take care!* Make straight for the end of the road, **Pico do Arieiro ★** (1818m/5963ft; 27km ▲✕☐☐

*You could turn left off this road above Terreiro da Luta, to go to Arieiro via the beautiful foresty road at Montado do Barreiro (☐; open daily from 08.00 to 19.00). It brings you out on the Arieiro road well above Poiso.

26

The Levada da Serra near the EN202 (Car tour 4; Walk 10 and Picnic 10)

WC *P*18; Walk 18; photograph pages 86-87). Visit too the **Miradouro do Juncal** (🚶 15min return; the path begins almost opposite the *pousada*): from here you have fine views over the sweep of the Metade Valley down to Faial and Penha de Águia ('Eagle Rock'). Later in the day, you will have another 'eagle's eye' view of the Metade, from Balcões. Return past the ice house ('Poço da Neve'; *P*17), where Walk 17 begins, and the meteorological station, and come again to Poiso (34km).

Now go straight ahead on the EN202 opposite — a moorland road and one of the loveliest on Madeira (🛱; *P*10). When you meet the EN102 (42km), turn left, passing the EN207 into Santo da Serra (🛒) and continuing up under deep shade to **Portela**★ (49km ✕🛒*P*14), where Walk 25 ends and Walk 14 begins. Here you enjoy the superb view to the north coast shown on pages 80-81, with Penha de Águia dominating the landscape.

From Portela take the EN101 north (🚗🛱). Walk 16, which explores a valley called 'Watch you don't fall!', begins at **Referta** (52.5km). Curl down into bright **Porto da Cruz** (55km ✕🛒⊕), where Walk 13 ends. A good viewpoint (🚗; photograph page 31) over the village is met on leaving, as you climb west to skirt the towering mass of Eagle Rock. Don't blink, or you might miss **Cruz** (57km; *P*15, 16), where Walk 15 starts and the ascent of Eagle Rock begins (Walk 16). Just before crossing the bridge over the Ribeira de São Roque, turn right up to a viewpoint (🚗) on the lower flanks of Penha de Águia, from where the photograph on pages 20-21 was taken. Return, cross the bridge (🚗) and pass the EN103 on your left (60km ✕). Skirt the centre of **Faial** (✕⊕) and make for Santana, for the present ignoring the two roadside viewpoints. The sun is now too high for this landscape to be seen at its best.

With good planning you will reach the Santana area late in the morning. Before entering the village centre, turn left (after 71km) on the EN101-5, signposted 'Achada do Teixeira/Queimadas'. Climb to the crossing of the Levada do Caldeirão Verde — it's just 250m below the forestry house at **Pico das Pedras** (✿🛱 with fireplaces). Short walk

The Porto Novo Valley near Assomada (Car tour 2, Walk 8 and Picnic 8). The late afternoon sun paints the escarpment burnished copper.

19 comes in here, and Walk 24 begins here. At the top of the road (⌖☎🅿) you reach the **Achada do Teixeira ★** (79km ☎🅿), where Walk 18 ends and Walk 23 begins. If you have time for a *leisurely* picnic, you can choose Queimadas Park (🏠🅿✿*P*19; photographs pages 23, 32, 92) or Homem em Pé/Pico Ruivo (*P*23). To picnic at Homem em Pé or on the Ruivo path (🅿), park here at the Achada. To picnic at Queimadas*, park by the levada passed earlier. (Although the EN101-5 was signposted to Queimadas, you can only *walk* to Queimadas Park from this road.)

On your return from the Achada do Teixeira, continue to **Santana ★** (93km ⛰✕🅿⊕), where Walk 19 ends. The island's 'most picturesque village' is an enchantment of thatched cottages, wayside flowers, patchwork-quilt gardens, and orchards, set below spectacular mountains. Break for lunch here, if you didn't bring a picnic. Then decide whether you have time to press on to São Jorge or the viewpoint at Arco (☎🅿✕), returning the same way. Ideally you want to be leaving Santana at about 15.00.

Return to Faial. It's now afternoon, and you are just in time to enjoy the best views from the two *miradouros* (☎) west of the village. Clouds scud across the sky, creating fascinating mosaics of light and shade on this dramatic landscape. Eagle Rock is seen from base to summit, standing guard over church and village, at the confluence of three great river valleys: the Metade, the Seca and the São Roque. This superb panorama is likely to be one of your most lasting impressions of Madeira.

As you climb out of **Faial**, turn right on the EN103 (102km ✕). Look left to see São Roque atop its *lombo* — the spine separating the parallel ravines of the São Roque and Metade rivers — as you follow the road up the spectacularly-terraced Seca Valley as far as the tiny hamlet of **Cruzinhas** (107km), where Walk 24 ends.

*Just over 1km west of the Achada do Teixeira road on the EN101, an old cobbled road leads steeply uphill to Queimadas Park, where Walks 19, 20 and 21 begin. Once you're on this narrow, poorly-paved road, there's nowhere to turn round and few passing places. It's usually easier to walk to Queimadas from Pico das Pedras (30 minutes each way), unless you're lucky enough to come when the road is newly tarred.

Just after you cross the Metade, a rough road leads right to the power station at Fajã da Nogueira (Walk 22). Climb past the fruit trees of **Cedro Gordo** and forests of cedar, cypress, pine and eucalyptus, to the gentle environs of Ribeiro Frio. There are several well-placed picnic sites (🍴) along the way, before you come to a viewpoint (📷) left over the valley. Soon reach the sweet coolness of **Ribeiro Frio ★** (112km 🍴🍴❀), where Walk 25 begins. Take a break here to walk to the **Balcões** — ('Balconies'; *P*25; 40min return). The signposted path is just below the souvenir shop. Follow it beside the dry levada; in 20 minutes you'll pass through a cut in the towering, moss-covered basalt and find yourself high in the Metade Valley. Soon come to a fork, where the old levada goes left; turn right and you're at the Balcões in a minute. It's a view to contrast with that from the Juncal *miradouro* visited earlier in the day. Eagle Rock is seen again, presiding over the north coast villages. But from the Balcões (see photograph page 19) the jagged central peaks dominate the scene. The Metade takes its source on these heights, and its tributaries feed the power station 250m/820ft below you (Walk 22), from where the Tornos Levada flows on to irrigate the southeast.

Just beyond the souvenir shop are the trout hatcheries and small botanical gardens. There are more picnic tables (🍴) as you climb round and round out of Ribeiro Frio, through a conifer forest, to meet again the moorlands of Poiso (118km). There's one more road to be explored: the EN203, a forestry road signposted left to Camacha, 0.5km south of Poiso. This delightful route overlooks Gaula's church and the Deserta Islands. When you lose the moorland to gorse, ferns and pine, you cross the Levada da Serra at Paradise Valley (Short walk 10-2). Half a kilometre further on, meet the EN102 (122km 🍴). Turn right for Funchal.

The Levada Calheta—Ponta do Pargo (Walk 31)

5 PORTO MONIZ AND THE PAÚL DA SERRA

Funchal • Ribeira Brava • São Vicente • Seixal • Porto Moniz • Ribeira da Janela Valley • Paúl da Serra • Bica da Cana • Encumeada • Funchal

158km/98mi; 7-8 hours' driving; Exit B from Funchal (plan page 10)

On route: ⊞ at Campanário, Vinháticos, Encumeada, Chão dos Louros, Fonte do Bispo, Rabaçal; Picnics (see **P** symbol and pages 12-15): (6), 26, 28, (32, 33a-e), (35); Walks: 4, 6, 23, 26-30, (32, 33) 34, (35)

This is the easiest tour to the west of the island and combines especially well with the 'Mountains' circuit (Tour 4), to provide a two-day programme covering almost all of Madeira's best landscapes, without any duplication of routes. The southwest coastal road is well worth pursuing (see Car tour 6), but it is a very long route — especially for those based at Matur/Machico. Expect busy roads as far as Ribeira Brava. You will also have to go slowly on the narrow corniche road between São Vicente and Porto Moniz — where you may encounter tour coaches (but they usually ply this route in the afternoon, which is a good reason for you to be there in the **morning** *— in addition to seeing the corniche in the best light). Watch out for pot-holes!*

F ollow Car tour 1 to **São Vicente** (55km). North of the village, turn left on the justly-famed corniche road to Porto Moniz: for 15 kilometres it soars up cliffs and swoops down again to the sea, racing in single-minded determination through tunnels and waterfalls. *Drive carefully; sound your horn at blind corners; lights on in the tunnels.* (The edge of the road is usually built up with solid concrete; motorists should not find it vertiginous.)

There are three viewpoints (👁) on the route. The first is at a tunnel 2km east of **Seixal** (63km ✄⊕), a village perched high on a promontory, where a graceful church looks out over terrifyingly-steep vineyards. It is said that the feathery heath tree hedges here not only protect the

The lighthouse at Ponta do Pargo (Car tour 6) and the village of São João, from the Levada Calheta—Ponta do Pargo (Walk 31)

Descending into Porto da Cruz: the eastern headlands, setting for Walk 13, stretch to the distant arm of São Lourenço (Car tour 4).

crops from the wind, but the farmers from falling into the sea… The next viewpoint is at another tunnel, just after you pass *through* waterfalls. Here you look out east past Seixal, as far as São Jorge; in the foreground, the falls cascade over towering cliffs where 'Pride of Madeira' clings tenaciously. West lies **Ribeira da Janela**: village and river take their name from the 'window' (*janela*) in the lava rock off the shore. Just past the mouth of the river is the final outlook (📷) over this dramatic coastal landscape; then round a bend, and you are in **Porto Moniz ★** (72km ▲ △ ✗ ⛽ ⊕ ⊼). Here reefs in the coastal lava rocks create a maze of glassy sea water pools where you can swim or picnic — if you don't mind the cool breezes. If you haven't brought a picnic, break for lunch here.

Climbing out of Porto Moniz on the steep hairpin bends of the EN101, you'll find two bird's-eye viewpoints (📷) over the village setting. Just 3.5km up from the roundabout by the petrol station, you pass the road off left to Walk 35 (*P*35) and then meet the EN204 southeast (in 78km, by the cattle market). Turn left and follow this road along the course of Madeira's greatest valley. The far-off views over the north and south coasts are splendid. But even more impressive is the size and magnificence of the Janela ravine. Virgin forests of heath and laurel cloak the mountainsides like coats of green sable.

You'll pass several good lookouts (📷) on the road: one of the finest is the old ruined 'Casa do Elias' at Quebradas (83km), from where there is a superb view over the village of Ribeira da Janela on its conical hilltop. Soon come to

The fairytale setting of Queimadas Park (Picnic 19, Walks 19-21)

another *miradouro* near **Fonte do Bispo** (89km 📷🏠), from where the EN210 runs south down to Prazeres. If you have binoculars, looking southeast you can see the Rabaçal houses at the head of the valley ... and even the Risco waterfall. Across the valley, on a hill, find a curiously bare area, studded with trees. This is the idyllic Fanal, where some of the island's indigenous laurels are still to be found (Walk 34; photograph page 128). Beyond the Fanal, the peaks in the east rise above cloud necklaces. The lighthouse at Ponta do Pargo is glimpsed in the west.

At 96km, past the EN211 south to Calheta (Alternative walk 33-1), you reach the head of the valley, by a reservoir. Here you are just above Rabaçal, a beauty spot much beloved by Madeirans. A detour down the *very narrow* road adds 4km to the tour (🏠🏠*P*33a-e).

Past the Rabaçal road, you approach the moorland vista of the **Paúl da Serra**, so very different from the Janela

Looking west from the Lombo do Mouro (Car tours 5 and 6, Walk 29)

Valley. Even in the rain the Paúl has a strange beauty: the moors take on a golden hue, the bracken throws up wine-red flames, and seagulls swirl over the marshes. On sunny days, the air is always bright as diamonds.

Beyond the signpost left 'Fanal/Ribeira da Janela' (Walk 34), you come to the EN208 south: Walk 32 and **P**32 begin 4km down this road. Bear left here (100.5km) for 'Bica da Cana/Estanquinhos', passing a statue to Nossa Senhora da Serra on the right. Then bear right at 102km for **Bica da Cana**. Just 1km beyond wind generators, two concrete pillars mark the stone-laid trail to this old lodge, on your left (104.5km ▲戸 and ☎ at the end of the track above the house; **P**28 and Alternative walk 28).

Continue on the EN204 for the breathtaking descent to Encumeada. You look out to the great peaks in the east, from the vantage point shown on pages 110-111. Some 4.5km from Bica da Cana, you pass above the Lombo do Mouro house, where Walk 29 joins the levada. Then, 1km further on, you pass a signpost on the left: 'Encumeada/Bica da Cana'; Walk 28 begins its climb to Pináculo here. Soon you skirt above the magnificent Levada do Norte and its 'tributary', the Levada das Rabaças, and you follow them to **Encumeada** (114km 🗪戸✕).

From here retrace your outgoing route to Funchal.

6 THE SUNNY SOUTHWEST COAST

Funchal • Ribeira Brava • Canhas • Arco da Calheta • Prazeres • Raposeira • (Paúl do Mar) • Ponta do Pargo • (Porto Moniz) • Ribeira da Janela Valley • Bica da Cana • Encumeada • Funchal

*181km/112mi; 8-9 hours' driving **without detours**; Exit B from Funchal (plan page 10). A diversion to the coast at Faja da Ovelha is recommended (add 16km/10mi) ... and you may want to go on to Porto Moniz for lunch, if you didn't bring a picnic (add 14km/9mi).*

On route: 戸 at Campanário, Ponta do Sol, Prazeres, east of Raposeira, Fonte do Bispo, Rabaçal; Picnics (see **P** symbol and pages 12-15): (6), 26, 28, (31, 32, 33a-e), (35); Walks 4, 23, 26-31, (32, 33), 34, (35)

This tour is described from the vantage point of the EN101. The roads are all asphalted but, if you find endless sorties into and out of valleys irksome, you can take the direct coastal road (EN213) between Ribeira Brava and Calheta ... of course you will miss the fine views that you have from the higher EN101.

The notes for Car tour 1 (page 17) will take you to **Ribeira Brava** (31km), where you bear right inland off the esplanade and then left over the bridge, to climb the EN101. Pass the road down to Tabua and then the starting point for Walk 30 (at the third bus stop, after you round the point). Soon Lombada da Ponta do Sol (♦) is signposted up to the right; sugar-cane plantations flourished in this area in the 1500s. The road (☞♯) continues above Ponta do Sol (✕☒⊕♯ and ♦ founded in the 15th century); it's worth a 1km detour down left into the village for morning coffee.

Go on through pretty **Canhas** (41km ♦ ✕☒). Just beyond the church, on the right, notice the first of fourteen statues representing the Stations of the Cross; after the last, on a straight stretch of road (☒), there is a monument to St Theresa (♦). Opposite is the taxi rank (if you are dropping off passengers for Walk 32) and, not far along, the EN208 heads up right to the Paúl da Serra. Soon you come to two dramatic viewpoints straight down over the sparkling houses and banana trees of Madalena do Mar (▲✕), 450m/1475ft below (☞ and ☞♯).

Interesting churches, where some artefacts remain from the days of their founding, are to be found at the three Calhetas. The first is the Manueline **Loreto** chapel (♦) on the outskirts of **Arco da Calheta**. It's on your left, on the main road, just past a road up right to a viewpoint (☞) at Pico do Arco. Walk 32 ends here. The next is the 15th-century mother church in Calheta (♦▲✕☒⊕), 3km south of the EN101. The third is the 16th-century Reis Magos Chapel at Estreito da Calheta (♦✕), also below the road.

Climb under mimosa to **Prazeres** (65km ▲♯) and continue to **Raposeira** (69km). Just west of the church, you could take a detour, turning left down the *very narrow* cobbled lane, to a viewpoint over Paúl do Mar, 600m/2000ft below (*P*31; photograph page 17). Soon the main road carries you to the turning left to this seaside village (EN212 via Fajã da Ovelha, at 70km; ♯). If you have time, this detour is highly recommended: the descent is spectacular, and you will see some fine basalt chimneys in the rock before you reach the village, where sea-spray foams up over the quay. Return to the main road and turn left.

The main tour bypasses these viewpoints, to make straight for **Ponta do Pargo** (79km; photograph page 30). The *second*, tarred road to the left leads to the lighthouse (81km ☞), from where the views are mesmerising. Waves weave endless variations of lacy patterns against the rocks, 300m/1000ft straight below you. The cliffs are a riot of poppies and thistles. From this most westerly point on Madeira, continue for some 16km to the EN204 and bear right … or first go on to Porto Moniz for lunch.

Then see notes on page 31 (Car tour 5) to end the tour.

✺ Walking

In this Fourth edition we've added many walks, including some easily accessible from Machico, and overprinted the routes on Portuguese military maps. We trust that these maps will give you a far better feeling for the terrain and help you identify many more landmarks than was possible on the maps Pat drew for the earlier editions. We've shown where walks link up on all the maps, so that you can make up your own walk combinations, but please: use the footpaths we've highlighted in green, or roads or tracks (see 'Guides ... maps' below).

Beginners: Many walks are suitable for you. Start with those described as easy, and be sure to check all the short and alternative walks — some are easy versions of the long walks for experts. Look, too, at the picnic suggestions.

Experienced walkers: If you are accustomed to rough terrain and have a head for heights, you should be able to take most of the walks in this book in your stride. Provided, of course, that storm damage or bulldozing has not made the way unsafe, and *provided that you follow the route as we describe it.* If you have not reached one of our landmarks after a reasonable time, you must go back to the last 'sure' point and start again.

Experts: You should manage all the walks easily, *provided that you are used to very sheer unprotected drops* (some levada paths give virtually no respite from constant 'exposure'). We've also alerted you to other walks you might tackle: these are usually indicated in footnotes.

It is important that *all* walkers, whether beginners or experts, read and *heed* the country code on page 128.

G uides, waymarking, maps

Walks graded 'expert' may also be done by experienced walkers in the company of a **guide** who knows the route. These walks may be prone to heavy mists or especially vertiginous or hazardous under certain conditions. For example, you cannot 'get lost' on the north coast path between Boca do Risco and Porto da Cruz, but only someone who knows that path well will know if a landslide is too recent to be crossed. The same applies to levadas: when it is too dangerous to continue beside the channel, you may not realise that a path must be found to skirt around a narrow place or an obstruction. Some taxi drivers act as guides; enquire also at the Tourist Office.

There is hardly any **waymarking** on the island although, since the publication of this book, a few of the most popular routes have been sporadically signposted.

For all the routes described in these notes, the **maps** we've reproduced are the most useful you will find. We have updated and annotated large-scale military maps issued in the 1960s. We've added new roads, but remember: we haven't been able to *delete* the many old paths and trails indicated, *many of which are no longer viable!* If we know that a path *is* viable, we have marked it with a dotted green line, even though the route may not be described in the book.

Where to stay

If you are going to Madeira purely for a walking holiday, we'd suggest that you spend one week in **Funchal** (to enjoy the walks in the south- and northeast of the island) and a week at the beautifully-situated **Pousada dos Vinháticos** (from where you can quite easily get to the walks in the centre and west of Madeira).

If you have only a week, or if walking is not your top priority, then it's best to stay in Funchal. The bus network radiates from the capital, affording all the best connections. All our walks are written up based on Funchal. However, judicious use of the timetables at the back of the book will enable you to join a walk from wherever you are based. There is currently **accommodation** at Santana, Boaventura, São Vicente, Seixal, Porto Moniz, Santa, Prazeres, Calheta, Ribeira Brava, Vinháticos, Arieiro, and Camacha, as well as in the tourist areas of Funchal, Caniço and Machico.

The only **camping** area is at Porto Moniz.

Rest house accommodation should be booked well in advance, in writing.*

---

*For the **Pico Ruivo** rest house, write to the Tourist Office, Avenida Arriaga, 9000 Funchal. For the government rest houses at **Rabaçal, Bica da Cana** and **Queimadas**, write to the Gabinete do Presidente, Quinta Vigia, 9000 Funchal. In both cases, state the house in which accommodation is required, number of nights and number of persons. You can also book during your visit (note that the Quinta Vigia is No. 13 on our town plan), but the government rest houses are likely to be fully booked. All rest houses provide bedding and cooking facilities. Take your own provisions and remember that all are in the mountains: there is no heating except for open fires. It may also be possible to stay at some **forestry houses** (Pico das Pedras, etc) — enquire on booking.

Weather

Madeira has fine walking weather the year round, although summer is most reliable (and usually not too hot). Equinoctial rains can be expected in late September/October and in March/April, but there will be many fine days as well. June, when the island is often covered by a 'hood' of low-lying clouds (the *capaçete*), is the only month best avoided.

Safe walking demands accurate reading of the weather signs and common sense. Outside summer many walks, especially in the north and west, can be treacherous. Even on the most glorious winter's day, levada paths will be full to overflowing and some mountain trails like waterfalls. For this reason, **we recommend that you do not undertake any walk graded 'expert' in winter**, no matter how fine the day. And bear in mind that other walks, especially in the north and west, might be very wet and hazardous.

Apart from the seasons, Madeira's weather is determined by **wind direction**. Whatever the season, the weather will be at its best with a light northeasterly (trade) wind. If the wind swings round to west or (worst of all) southwest, unsettled weather follows. The central mountains catch up the clouds carried by these winds; read the signs to find the best 'microweather' for your walk:

■ **Strong winds** from any direction except east, bring rain, if not storms. (Eg, if a strong northeasterly blows in, we head for the southwest.)

■ **Strong wind from the east or south of east (*leste*)**: This hot, dry wind from Africa guarantees good walking everywhere, with crystal clear views on the heights.

■ **Mild winds from any direction except south or southwest** afford good walking all round the island.

■ **Mild winds from the south/southwest** bring rain!

■ As a rule of thumb, the **Deserta Islands** can serve as a 'ready-reckoner' for weather signs:

— If they are clearly visible (wind from W of N): the southeast, northeast and east are clear — at least in the valleys. The west is cloudy.

— If they are hardly visible (wind from the E, SE): the south may be cloudy, but walking is generally good everywhere.

— If they are cloudy (wind from the NE): the west, southwest and northwest are clear; eastern areas may be cloudy.

— If they seem very close and there is a white line on the horizon (wind from S, SW): rain is coming within 24 hours.

■ The general pattern is a clear morning, with clouds gathering by mid-day, and the sky clearing again by mid-afternoon. **Early starts are recommended!** Telephone 150 for a recorded weather forecast (in Portuguese).

What to take

If you are already on Madeira and haven't walking boots or a torch or rucksack, you can still do many of our walks. But don't attempt the more difficult ones without proper equipment. For each walk in this book, we tell you the *minimum* equipment necessary. Where we require walking boots, there is *no substitute*: you will need to rely on the grip and ankle support they provide, as well as their waterproof qualities. For all other walks wear stout lace-up shoes with thick rubber or 'Vibram'-type soles, to provide good grip. Do *not* venture on walks requiring a torch unless you have one — some levada tunnels are exceedingly long, and you *must* be able to see both the roof (for possible projections) and the path, because the water in the channel may be very deep, cold, and fast-moving.

You may find the checklist below useful:

walking boots (which must be broken-in and comfortable)
waterproof rain gear (outside summer months)
plastic bottle and water purifying tablets
torch (preferably throwing a *wide* beam)
long sleeved shirt (sun protection)
long trousers, tight at the ankles
first-aid kit, including bandages

anorak (zip opening)
knives and openers
2 light cardigans
bus timetable (see page 9)
sunhat, suncream, sunglasses
plastic rainhat
extra pair of socks and bootlaces
'Dog Dazer' (see 'Nuisances')
plastic groundsheet
plastic plates, cups, etc
whistle, compass

Please bear in mind that we've not done *every* walk in this book under *all* weather conditions: we may not realise just how hot — or wet — some walks might be. Walking boots are *always* more useful than shoes, and we wear them all year round. In hot weather, *always* carry a long-sleeved shirt as well as your sunhat, and take your lunch in a shady spot. We rely on your good judgement to modify our equipment lists according to the season.

Nuisances

Dogs are not often a problem, but we find the 'Dog Dazer' a good investment. For details about this ultra-sonic dog deterrent write to: Dazer UK, Freepost, London SW11 6BR. The same firm offers handy personal alarms, far more effective than a whistle, for whatever use.

Begging children have, frankly, become a menace. We *never*, under any circumstances, give them anything but a greeting. Obviously some walkers have given in to the blackmail, which has just aggravated the problem.

New roads have ruined many walks on the island.

While there seems little need for some of them (such as Paúl da Serra/Ribeira da Janela), you have only to watch the inhabitants of Curral carrying cinder building blocks for a new house up hundreds of steps to realise how selfish it is to deplore these roads. Pat was unable to lift even one of them, yet we saw a woman shouldering three and a man with four on his back — about 150 lbs, we reckoned.

P ortuguese for walkers

Once you venture off the beaten track, few of the older people speak English (the children often speak English or French). We have found an almost foolproof way to ask *and understand* directions in Portuguese. First, memorise the key questions and all their possible answers below; then **always phrase your questions so that you will get a yes ('sengh') or no ('nough') answer.**

KEY QUESTIONS (English/approximate Portuguese pronunciation)

'Please, sir (madam).	**Fahz** fah-**vohr**, sehn-**yohr** (sehn-**yoh**-rah).
Where is the levada to ...	**Ohn**-deh eh al leh-**vah**-dah **pah**-rah ...
(the main road to ...,	(ah ish-**trah**-dah **pah**-rah ...,
the footpath to ...,	ah veh-**ray**-dah **pah**-rah ...,
the way to ...,	oh cah-**mee**-noh **pah**-rah ...,
the bus stop)?	ah pah-**rah**-jeng)?
Many thanks.'	**Mween**-toh o-bree-**gah**-doh (to a woman say: '**Mween**-toh o-bree-**gah**-<u>dah</u>).

POSSIBLE ANSWERS (English/approximate Portuguese pronunciation)

here/there	ah-**key**/ah-**lie**
straight ahead/behind	**semp**-reh engh **frenght**/ ah-**trahs**
to the right/to the left	ah deh-**ray**-tah/ah ish-**kehr**-dah
above/below	engh **see**-mah/engh **bye**-joh

Ask a native speaker (your hotel porter, tour rep, or taxi driver) to help you with the pronunciation of these key phrases, as well as *place names*.

When you have your mini-speech memorised, always ask the many questions you can concoct from it in such a way that a yes/no answer will result. *Never* ask an open-ended question such as 'Where is the main road?' Even if you are standing on it, you probably won't understand the answer! Instead, ask the question and then **suggest the most likely answer yourself**, for example:

'**Fahz** fa-**vohr**, sehn-**yoh**-rah. **Ohn**-deh eh ah ish-**tra**-dah **pah**-rah Foon-**shal**? Eh **sem**-preh engh **frenght**?' *or* '**Fahz** fa-**vohr**, sehn-**yor**. **Ohn**-deh eh ah Le-**vah**-dah dohs **Tor**-nohs? Eh engh **see**-mah ah deh-**ray**-tah?'

An inexpensive phrase book will help you compose other 'key' phrases and answers. It is always pleasant to greet people you meet on your walks with a 'good morning' or 'good afternoon' (bohm **dee**-ah, boah **tard**).

Organisation of the walks

Our thirty-five main walks are grouped in three general areas: the southeast; the northeast and the great peaks; the west and northwest. We urge you to walk in *each* of these three areas, in order best to sample the island's landscapes.

We hope that the book is set out so that you can plan your walks easily — depending on how far you want to go, your abilities and equipment, the season … and what time you are willing to get up in the morning!

You might begin by looking at the fold-out touring map between pages 16 and 17. Here you can see at a glance the overall terrain, the extent of the levada network, main and secondary roads, and the orientation of the walking maps in the text. Flipping through the book, you'll see that there is at least one photograph for each walk.

Having selected one or two potential excursions from the map and the photographs, turn to the relevant walk. At the top of the page you will find planning information: distance/time, grade, equipment, and how to get there. If the grade and equipment specifications are beyond your scope, don't despair! *We almost always suggest a short version of each walk* and, in most cases, these shorter walks are far less demanding of agility and equipment.

When you are on your walk, you will find that the text begins with an introduction to the overall landscape and then quickly turns to a detailed description of the route itself. The large scale maps (all 1:40,000) have been specially annotated and, where possible, set out facing the walking notes. Times are given for reaching certain key checkpoints. Giving times is always tricky, because they depend on so many factors, but the times we give are a little slower than those we actually make ourselves. **Note that they do not include any stops!** Allow extra time for picnics, photography, and any other breaks.

Many of the **symbols on our walking maps** are self-explanatory, but below is a key to the most important:

RED — main or secondary road	best views	power station
=== track	600 height (metres)	spring or levada source (blue)
--- footpath	danger or danger of vertigo (red)	tank/tap (blue)
GREEN route of the walk	church/chapel	car/taxi parking
• • • or alternative	† statue	bus stop
BLUE levada	P picnic spot (see pages 12-15)	local bar/shop or café
]------[tunnel		

1 LEVADA DOS PIORNAIS: FUNCHAL • SOCORRIDOS VALLEY

Map page 44 and town plan pages 10-11; STOP PRESS page 136

Distance: 7km/4.3mi; 2h10min

Grade: easy, but sure-footedness is essential on a few short stretches, where there is also a **possibility of vertigo**.

Equipment: stout shoes, sunhat, picnic, water

How to get there: town 🚌 45 to the first stop *past* the stadium
To return: town 🚌 1 or 3 from Lombada back to Funchal centre

Short walks

1 Stadium — Madeira Palácio. 2.8km/1.7mi; 40min. Grade, equipment, access as above. Follow the main walk for 30min, then turn left down the Camino do Amparo (just before an electricity substation) to the EN101, opposite the Madeira Palácio. Return on any of the frequent town or country buses heading for Funchal centre.

2 Madeira Palácio — Lombada. 6km/3.7mi; 1h50min. Grade, equipment, return as above. Take any westbound bus to the Madeira Palácio. Climb the Caminho do Amparo, opposite the hotel, for ten minutes, to reach the levada — on your left, just before an electricity substation. Pick up the main walk at the 30min-point, adjusting times accordingly.

A 'citified' stroll with an astounding finish, at its best early in the morning or late in the afternoon — far too hot for midday. You stroll along a working, town levada. Babies are splashing in plastic tubs, while their mothers embroider tablecloths for the tourist shops in Funchal.

The bus drops you on the Rua dos Estados Unidos, just west of the stadium. **Start out** by walking back the way the

This walk affords marvellous views of Cabo Girão and the terraces on its eastern flanks. Should you experience some feelings of vertigo, there is usually room to walk on the other side of the levada (as you can see in the photograph). Below the levada lie some of the islands finest banana planta- tions; notice, on the other hand, how dry the land is above the water- course, where only the cacti thrive.

bus came for about 30m/yds. Then go down steps on your right; they take you to the levada. Turn right on the levada channel (don't continue to the bottom of the steps).

Within **15min** you can see the Lido, banana fields and the tourist zone of western Funchal. Soon you enjoy marvellous views of Cabo Girão and the terraces on its eastern flanks. Should you experience some feelings of vertigo, there is often room to walk on the other side of the levada, where you won't be so exposed to the drops.

In **30min**, at Amparo, two cobbled roads lead down to the EN101. At the second road, you must climb up a few paces to find the levada. (Short walk 1 leaves here and Short walk 2 joins here.) Now you are just south of São Martinho church, a landmark on so many island walks because of its especially graceful spire. In **55min** pass a road leading up sharp right to São Martinho. Then, in just over **1h**, after a long cinderblock wall on the left, you come to a road. Cross it to the electricity pylon opposite (which is also a bus stop). Here steps take you back down to the levada, covered by a concrete walkway. In a moment or two, a cobbled road joins. Follow it to a large house with decorative window tiles. At the left of the house are steps up to the levada.

In **1h10min** the levada seems to end in Quebradas. Climb steps up to a road and turn right on it. Then cross the road and bear left under the road bridge. Walk up to a 'stop' sign at the crossroad and turn left (signposted 'Camara de Lobos'), passing the school on your left. Beyond the school ignore the road to the left (over a bridge). In 10m/yds you pass a tap on your left; cross the road here and climb steps opposite to the levada.

In **1h30min** a cobbled road branches off left, and then a cobbled *path* in under **1h45min,** just before a level change in the levada. The walk ends five minutes later, above a small eucalyptus grove, from where there are superb views into the Socorridos Valley (*P*1; see photograph opposite). You could follow the levada for several minutes more, before it becomes unbearably vertiginous and disappears into some tunnels. If you *do* follow it a little further perhaps, like us, you will marvel at the golden curves of this watercourse hewn in the side of the rock … sheer sculpture.

Return to the cobbled path passed at 1h45min and follow the road adjacent to it for two minutes, down to Lombada (**2h10min**). Wait for the bus on the south side of the road, just at the bar (no *'paragem'* sign).

2 LEVADA DO CURRAL: SANTA QUITÉRIA • FAJÃ • SANTA QUITÉRIA

Distance: 8km/5mi; 2h10min

Grade: easy, but sure-footedness is essential on a few stretches, where there is also a **possibility of vertigo**, in spite of the protective railings.

Equipment: stout shoes, long trousers, sunhat, picnic, water

How to get there and return: town 🚌 8 or 16 from Funchal to Santa Quitéria and back, or 🚗: park well off the road in Santa Quitéria.

Alternative walk: Ribeira da Lapa detour. Before you descend the path to the rock pools at the 40min-point, keep along the levada (*provided that the protective railings are in place; this is one of the most dangerous passages on the island*). You will enter the upper reaches of the Ribeira da Lapa and will no doubt be as astonished as we were to find such an awesome place so close to Funchal. It is at Fajã, where the Ribeira da Lapa joins the Ribeira do Curral, that the two become the Socorridos. When you consider that its flow cut this valley and today feeds four *major* levadas, you can perhaps imagine what a torrent it was when Zarco first saw it! We suggest that you *end this detour* at the bottom of the steps climbing up into the waterfall: return to the path first reached at the 40min-point; this detour will have cost you 30min. Even if the railings are repaired (they were installed late 1991, but we found them partly broken in mid-1992), remember that it is much easier to climb *up* such vertiginous steps than to get down them again. If you *do* climb the steps, you will get soaked and will then have to pass through a tunnel (*torch and boots required*). Beyond the tunnel continue along the levada, watching carefully for a large blue ⌂ symbol on a rock on your right. Zigzag down the *very overgrown* path opposite this 'hat' symbol, to get down to Fajã (passing the two remaining telephone poles in the hamlet). Just beyond the lower telephone pole (7min down), find a burned-out, two-storey house, with roof tiles stacked up in its front garden. Turn left on the path just below this house, to get down to the rock pools and rejoin the main walk (this route also takes an extra 30min). (*It is very important that you use the path described, however overgrown it may be; it is the **only** real path at Fajã. Do not try to descend on any terraces; at the very least you will be lacerated by blackberry thorns.*)

The glorious basin of the Socorridos Valley, looking south from near Fajã. Walk 1, on the lower Levada dos Piornais, ends at the eucalyptus grove above the mouth of the river, which is also the setting for Picnic 1.

The Levada do Curral between Curral das Freiras and Funchal was once one of the most beautiful on the island — it was the inspiration for the First edition of this book. In 1992, however, the upper Socorridos Valley was devastated by forest fires. Not only is the beauty of the valley lost for many years to come, but the levada is no longer passable* north of Fajã, the deserted hamlet where we end this walk. Fortunately, the landscape south of Fajã was untouched by the conflagration.

Start out at the bus terminus in Santa Quitéria. Walk downhill (northwest) on tar for five minutes, passing the Travessa das Preces on your right and a shop/bar on your left. Then continue down a concrete drive for another few minutes, to join the levada (**8min**). Turn right and soon round the Ribeira do Arvoredo in a woodland glen. Some **25min** from Santa Quitéria the levada has taken you into the abundance of the Socorridos Valley — its richness of colour and form defying description and photography. Banana and sugar cane plantations sweep down to the sea, creating an abstract painting in every shade of green, caught in a frame of grape trellises and flowers.

In about **40min** you pass a solitary house on your right, full of flowers. Watch out for a good path on your left, barely a minute past this house. Follow it downhill to rock pools in the Ribeira da Lapa, from where you can look up into the fearsome gorge visited in the Alternative walk. Then continue on the good path up into fire-ravaged Fajã (**1h05min**) … perhaps to picnic, but certainly to ponder: *why* was this beautifully-situated hamlet deserted? And why so precipitously? (When we first 'discovered' it in 1974, there was still crockery on tables and linen on beds in some of the deserted cottages!)

Return the same way to pick up your bus in Santa Quitéria (**2h10min**) … or perhaps first follow the levada to the left for a short time, as suggested in the Alternative walk, to get a closer look at the awesome gorge.

*It is *imperative* that you do not attempt this walk without getting 'Update' information from us (see inside back cover). The fires destroyed all the trees along the levada, leaving the unprotected sheer drops of 400m/1300ft totally exposed. Rockfalls damaged the channel itself, breaking away the edge. We walked for about an hour north of Fajã, sometimes balancing on a precipice no more than 15cm/6" wide, only to find that landslides prevented us from getting to Curral. Of course, there is a *levadeiro* on duty repairing the channel seven days a week and, of course, *he* can manage the whole route, being half goat. But he told us that daily rock- and landslides were making his job almost impossible.

3 CORTICEIRAS • BOCA DOS NAMORADOS • CURRAL DAS FREIRAS

Map page 47; photograph page 24   **Distance:** 7.3km/4.5mi; 3h

Grade: expert. Steep ascent (330m/1100ft) and descent of 700m/2300ft on a narrow path littered with loose stones. **Danger of vertigo!**

Equipment: walking boots, long trousers, sunhat, picnic, water, whistle; extra cardigans and anorak in cool weather

How to get there: 🚌96 from Funchal to Corticeiras
To return: 🚌81 from Curral to Funchal

Short walk: Corticeiras — Boca dos Namorados — Corticeiras. 5.2km/ 3.2mi; 1h50min. Strenuous ascent, but stout shoes will suffice. Access as for main walk; return by 🚌96 from Corticeiras. Or 🚗 to Corticeiras (via Estreito): park at the Quinta Mis Muchachos, saving 15min each way.

T his is one of Madeira's 'classic' walks and, although the path periodically suffers fire and storm damage, it is always repaired. Superb views over Curral's setting accompany you beyond the Boca dos Namorados.

Start out with your back to the bar in Corticeiras. Turn left and follow the road southeast. Pass the electricity substation some 200m along, and bear left uphill beyond it. At a fork, go left again. In **15min** you reach the ruined Quinta Mis Muchachos on your right; take the track swinging uphill to the left opposite it. Ignore any side trails and, at a fork reached in ten minutes, be sure to go right. Keep on this main trail which is cobbled to within sight of the pass; it's an unrelenting climb of 330m/1100ft, but at least there is plenty of shade from the dense eucalyptus forest.

At the Boca dos Namorados ('Lovers' Pass'; **1h**) a wide forestry track crosses in front of you. Turn left on it, then immediately fork right downhill on a wide earthen path. Beyond a telephone pole (**1h10min**) the path dips into S-bends. Be sure to *stop* to enjoy the views over Curral's river and tortuous motor road; *the precipitous path, slippery and strewn with stones, requires your full attention.* In **1h30min** pass to the left of Pico do Cedro and, 20 minutes later, come to another knoll shaded by chestnuts and eucalyptus — both are fine picnic spots.

In **2h15min** you meet the first cultivated terraces and houses of Curral de Baixo. Be sure to go *left uphill* on a path *before* the first house. You come onto a concrete walkway: note the delightful flower-bound house on your right and its unusually-thatched *palheiro*. In **2h30min** cross a small levada and pass above the school (on your right). In **2h45min** concrete steps lead you down to the road. Cross the Ribeira do Curral (**3h**) and wait for the bus (no *'paragem'* sign) 20m/yds uphill, opposite the concrete steps … that only a masochist would climb to Curral!

4 BOCA DA CORRIDA • PICO GRANDE • ENCUMEADA

See also map on reverse of touring map and STOP PRESS page 136.

Distance: 14km/8.7mi; 4h15min

Grade: easy mountain walking as far as the Boca do Cerro, on a wide and grassy trail (see photograph page 48). Further on, however, the path is narrow, often wet, and *sometimes impassable* below Pico Grande, due to landslides. For this part of the walk, surefootedness is essential, and there is a **possibility of vertigo**.

Equipment: as Walk 3 opposite, plus plastic bottle and water purifying tablets

How to get there: 🚌 3, 4, 6, 7, 96, 107, 137, 139 or 154 from Funchal to Estreito de Câmara de Lobos; then taxi to Boca da Corrida (there is a fixed rate for the taxi journey, and it is high, because the road is very poor). *To return:* 🚌 6 from Encumeada to Funchal

Alternative walk: Boca da Corrida — Boca do Cerro — Corticeiras. 11.5km/7mi; 3h40min. Easy. Stout shoes, sunhat, picnic, water. Access as for main walk; return on 🚌 96 from Corticeiras to Funchal. Follow the main walk to Boca do Cerro and back; then descend to Corticeiras on the road from the forestry house (dotted green line on the map below). *Note: do not try to drive to Boca da Corrida; the road has deteriorated so much that you risk losing your transmission.*

If we had to choose our favourite mountain walk on the island, it would probably be this one. There is so much to recommend it: not only are the views magnificent throughout, but there's hardly any climbing! The first part of the walk follows a wide and grassy trail — easy walking for everyone. Rounding Pico Grande the going *can* be tricky, depending on the time of year and whether there have been any recent storms or fires, but most of the time the path is perfectly safe, and very few people will find it vertiginous.

Start out at the pass of Boca da Corrida, where there is a forestry house and a spectacular viewpoint over Curral das Freiras. Take the stone-laid trail heading off left *behind* the forestry house; almost at once turn right up steps bordered by wooden railings (there may be a signpost 'Curral das Freiras/Encumeada'). You climb a rough trail, heading for a fenced-in area. The route is very clear as it leads to the right of the fencing. After some **8min**, the walk levels out to reveal the central mountain ridge towering above Curral. Soon reach a promontory on the right: it points directly to our grassy trail and Pico Grande. It's John's favourite mountain and easily identified from all over the island because of the rocky protrusion on its summit. As the trail 'corkscrews' its way towards Pico Grande, be sure to avoid the crumbled old path down left to Serra de Água. Soon enjoy very fine views of Encumeada and the north, from the pass of Boca dos Corgos. Then, in **45min,** come to a gate at the Passo de Ares, from where you can look out west towards the vastness of the Paúl da Serra.

The old grassy trail, once the main north/south route over the island, is easy walking as far as the Boca do Cerro on the flanks of Pico Grande.

At **1h10min** reach another gate leading to the fourth pass, the Boca do Cerro, where the Alternative walk turns back.* Beyond the Boca do Cerro, our route (which was the main north/south trail over the island in the 1800s) is no longer wide and grassy, but it *is* easily discernible. Turn down left through the prickly gorse (you may find signposts here to Encumeada and Curral) and, soon, begin to skirt the awe-inspiring escarpment of Pico Grande. It will take twenty minutes to pass this rock face, where the *path is very narrow, often wet, and prone to landslides.* Then the generally narrow route begins its descent to Encumeada.

In **2h**, past the Fenda do Ferreiro, reach a wide promontory — an idyllic picnic spot. The views towards the Paúl da Serra and down to the Pousada dos Vinháticos (where you may be heading to spend the night) are especially fine. In **2h35min**, there is a U-turn in the path, where you *may* see a sign pointing back to Estreito. Be sure to head northeast, and ignore a second path down left ten minutes further on (**2h45min**; this is an alternative route to the EN104, if the valley is torn up by roadworks — see STOP PRESS, page 136). Five minutes later, you will come into the enchanting valley of the Ribeira do Poço, emerald green and bright with *poios* and *palheiros*.

Cross a grass-covered stone bridge in **3h**, and ignore two further paths down left (**3h25min**, **3h35min**). Soon, at **3h55min**, you come to the pipe carrying water from the Norte and Rabaças levadas (Walk 26) down to the power station at Serra de Água. Here you'll have to clamber some 3m/yds up to the roadworks, which you follow to the EN104 (**4h05min**). Wait for the bus here: flag it down! Alternatively, walk uphill to Encumeada and over the pass, for a view of the north coast (**4h15min**), or head downhill to the Pousada dos Vinháticos (**4h45min**).

*From the Boca do Cerro *experts* can scramble to the summit of Pico Grande (1h30min return) or descend to Curral (3h). The Pico Grande path forks left off the Curral path, to climb the eastern flanks of the mountain, but it soon disappears, and you must make your own way to the top. *Reckon on mists! Set up markers for your descent!* And be sure, if you climb to Pico Grande's summit, that you can get down again! Both this descent, and the descent to Curral, involve short stretches on narrow ledges — plenty of 'exposure'. One of us invariably sits down on the first ledge, contemplates the abyss below, and then finds that she can not go on — to the great disgust of the other, who she also forbids to proceed on his own. Both paths are viable for *expert* mountain walkers with a head for heights (friends and correspondents have followed them without difficulty) but remember: there are *no* protective railings at the exposed points. These routes are shown on the map by dotted green lines.

5 FONTES • ACHADA DA PINTA • TROMPICA • FONTES

Map on reverse of touring map **Distance:** 11km/6.8mi; 3h35min

Grade: moderate climb and descent of 500m/1650ft on track. The initial ascent is tiring in hot weather.

Equipment: stout shoes (walking boots preferable), sunhat, picnic, water; extra cardigan and anorak in cool weather

How to get there and return: 🚌 to Fontes, above Boa Morte. Turn off the EN101 at Barreiras, by the KM172 marker. Beyond Boa Morte, cross the Levada do Norte in the pine forest, then continue north. Round the deep valley of the Ribeira Funda and come to a village with a modern church, built in the same style as Ribeira Brava's. This is São Paulo; Fontes is the *next* hamlet, some 1km north. Fontes is also accessible by 🚐 127 from Ribeira Brava (leaves from behind the petrol station, at the east end of the promenade), but current times are inconvenient, and there is no return bus. New buses may be added to this route; check with Rodoeste, the operator, either at their kiosk in Funchal or their station (No 35 on the town plan pages 10-11). You might also be able to return from Campanário; see notes at the bottom of page 52.

Alternative walk: Fontes — Achada da Pinta — Trompica — Boca da Corrida — Corticeiras. 15.5km/9.6mi; 4h45min. Especially recommended for those who wish to travel by bus. Moderate, but surefootedness is essential on the path in the Ribeira do Campanário. Equipment as above, but walking boots and long trousers recommended. Access as above; return by 🚐 96 from Corticeiras. At the Trompica forestry house, climb up the earthen bank at the left of the track, to find a good but narrow path which circles the Ribeira do Campanário. If you come to any forks, be prepared to spend a few minutes searching out the correct, well-trodden path (it may be overgrown, depending on the season) and remember not to lose height. Some 20min from Trompica you'll be at the centre of the valley, with a photogenic cultivated knoll below you. Soon there is a delightful grove above the path, on the left. Two river tributaries, with lovely rock pools, are crossed on stepping stones and, in 40min, you reach the lowest of the 'Casas do Dr Alberto' (you will have spotted the three buildings on the property on your approach). Here climb straight ahead, at the left-hand side of this lowest stone shed. You come to the highest building, where you meet a track. Turn right on this track for Boca da Corrida. Another track comes in from above you, on your left, in about 1h10min, and you reach the forestry house at Boca da Corrida 1h40min from Trompica. From here descend the cobbled road to Corticeiras (see green dotted line on the map page 47; allow 1h15min). *Special note: The path in the Campanário Valley is grazed by cows; we have often encountered up to a dozen on the narrow path. Be prepared to lose time here, shooing them away* **quietly***. Always go quietly in this valley which is* **not** *yet frequented by walkers. Approach the Casas do Dr Alberto quietly, too: one of the houses is inhabited and the lands are farmed by a charming man. Please protect the friendly welcome you will receive here for future walkers.*

Here's a walk that shows you the great divide formed by the Ribeira Brava from a new perspective. Not only will you have fantastic views over the north/south cleft of this deep ravine, but the panorama encompasses all the great peaks (Walks 18 and 23), Pico Grande (Walk 4), *and* the entire eastern escarpment of the Paúl da Serra, setting

*'Pride of Madeira' embellish
a rural cottage.*

for levada walks 26-29. What's more, this is one of the very few island walks that we can whole-heartedly recommend as a varied and satisfying circuit for those with hired cars.

Leave your transport at Fontes, well off the road (so that the bus can turn round). At the right-hand side of the bar/shop you will see a dirt track rising straight ahead and a track (or road) descending slightly, to the right of it. **Start out** by climbing the dirt track on the left. It's a steep haul, especially in hot weather, and there is *no shade*. But *don't* be discouraged by the dusty climb; once you reach the first pass, the way will become grassy and remain so for most of the walk.

The route takes you up the right-hand side of the Ribeira Grande. Within **35min** you will have crossed the Ribeiro Frio and be aiming for the first pass. On reaching it, the way becomes grassy. Look back to see the village of São Paulo (the one below Fontes): its church, although small and modern, is built in the style of Ribeira Brava's. Small herds of cows will be encountered throughout the walk, all grazing freely on this relatively level terrain.

Within **50min**, at another pass, you begin to enjoy the best views on the walk — the Ribeira Brava basin comes

Approaching the second pass on the walk, the great divide comes into view, and you look down towards Ribeira Brava's basin beyond a sea of thistles and foxgloves.

into sight, as well as the Lombo do Mouro (Walk 29), Vinháticos, Pináculo (Walk 28), and Encumeada. As you round Pico da Cruz (**1h**) be sure to bear right (due south) on the track, where a path descends to the left. The grassy track takes you through fields of spring-blooming thistles, foxgloves and broom; a meadow lies below. In the past barley was grown up here (the reason for cutting the track), but it did not flourish. Yet another pass, reached in **1h10min**, opens up views to the great peaks, from Grande round to Ruivo, via Pico do Gato and the Torres.

Beyond another pass, at about **1h25min**, you come to a Y-fork. The track to the right is the return route but, for the moment, go straight ahead, through a gate. Fifteen minutes later (**1h40min**), another fence is encountered; here a makeshift style must be negotiated. Seven minutes later the track makes a 90° turn to the left and ends at a pass (**1h50min**). Here climb up half right towards the summit, on no particular path. You will reach a small rock enclosure within seven minutes. At the far right-hand corner, stones have been placed to allow you to climb over *carefully*, without disturbing the wall. Inside the enclosure is a triangulation point (1430m on the map), where a blue ⌂ is painted on the concrete — a fanatical Madeiran walker's way of saying 'Kilroy was here' (you will see these 'blue hats' on almost all your walks). From here you have a new outlook — over Curral's setting and even down to Funchal. This is the Achada da Pinta (note that the military map incorrectly locates it further south).

Leave the triangulation point by climbing over the wall where you came in and retrace yours steps to the fork first met in 1h25min (about **2h25min**). Turn down sharp left. The track takes you down through a couple of gates and past minor tracks to the right and the left, which you ignore. By **2h45min** you're descending beneath sweet chestnuts and eucalyptus, but the track is no longer grassy. Five minutes later (**2h50min**) the Trompica forestry house is met, on your right. (Here the Alternative walk leaves us, by taking the path up to the left of the track.) Continue down past the forestry house on the track. Allow 40 minutes for the tedious return to Fontes. Some 20 minutes below Trompica, pass a small road off right to Terreiros. Ten minutes later, meet a major fork, where roadworks decend left to Lugar da Serra and Campanário (this would be handy for walkers travelling by bus; see touring map). Bear *right* here; the track descends a bit, before climbing gently back to Fontes (**3h35min**).

6 LEVADA DO NORTE: ESTREITO DE CÂMARA DE LOBOS • CAMPANÁRIO • BOA MORTE • BARREIRAS

Distance: 21km/13mi; 6h

Grade: easy, but some narrow places throughout. The stretch between Quinta Grande and Campanário (**possibility of vertigo**) is *only recommended for surefooted walkers with a head for heights.*

Equipment: stout shoes, sunhat, picnic, water, *torch*; extra cardigan and anorak in cool weather

How to get there: 🚌 96 from Funchal to the levada crossing, north of Estreito; ask for the 'Levada do Norte' bus stop.

To return: 🚌 4, 6, 7, 80, 107, 139 or 150 from Barreiras to Funchal

Short walks

1   Estreito — first waterhouse. 6.5km/4mi; 1h40min. Easy. Equipment and access as main walk. Follow the main walk for 1h40min; you will come to the EN101 where you can catch one of the above buses.

2   Quinta Grande — Campanário. 8km/5mi; 2h15min. Grade and equipment as main walk; **possibility of vertigo.** Access: 🚌 4, 6, 7, 80, 107, 123, or 139 from Funchal to 'Ribeira da Quinta Grande', where the EN101 crosses the levada. Follow the main walk from the 2h10min-point to the 3h30min-point, where you can follow the dirt track down to Campanário to catch 🚌 4, 6, 7, 80, 107, 123, 139 or 150.

3   Boa Morte circuit. 3.5km/2.2mi; 1h. Easy; *highly recommended for beginners or people with hired cars.* Wear sensible shoes and take a picnic. Access/ return: 🚌 6, 7, 107, 139 or 150 from Funchal to Ribeira Brava, then 🚌 127 to Boa Morte (leaves from behind the petrol station, at the east end of the promenade). From Boa Morte follow the road uphill to the levada in the pine forest. Turn right to see the waterhouse with its charming gardens, then follow the levada west, picking up the notes for the main walk at the 4h10min-point. You'll be back in Boa Morte in time for 🚌 148 to Funchal. 🚐 : If travelling by car, you can park beside the levada. Turn off the EN101 at Barreiras, by the KM172 marker.

All year round, this is a superb walk, with a sun-blessed aspect, through landscape rich in cultivation, thanks to the waters of the Levada do Norte (see notes in Walk 26). Here in early autumn the grapes are harvested for some of Madeira's best-known wines, and the valleys are thick with sugar cane and cherry trees.

When the bus roars up the hill at Estreito, you'll first pass the church and then a small chapel on the left. Just round the next bend is the bus stop, called 'Levada (do Norte)'. **The walk starts just here,**

Boa Morte's pine forest: you can picnic here, or follow the levada northwest, to overlook the valley of the Ribeira Brava (see photograph page 56). Picnic 6.

on the west side of the road, where you climb a few steps up to the levada — hidden under concrete at first, and covered by vine-bearing trellises. You'll hear it singing underfoot and reach the end of the covered walkway in **7min** at the most. Look left soon for good views of São Martinho Church and, on a clear day, the Deserta Islands. At about **20min** into the walk, be sure to look out for a path down and round a dangerous part of the levada. Soon you'll find yourself in the narrow valley of the Ribeira da Caixa, smothered in cherry blossoms in spring (do be sure to try some Madeiran cherry wine — *ginjinha* — during your visit). Perhaps take a break near the abandoned stone cottage reached in **30min** or the bridge at the head of the valley (**50min**).

On leaving the valley, start counting churches to measure your progress. At **1h05min** here's the first, below at Garachico. A charming blue and white waterhouse is met at **1h35min**. Its surrounds are generally locked. If so, walk to the front of the waterhouse, where you will meet a cobbled road, with cobbled steps inset into its west side. Climb these to regain the levada. In five minutes, cross the main road (**1h40min**). You can leave the walk here by taking any eastbound bus (Short walk 1).

Staying on the levada, and drawing ever closer to Cabo

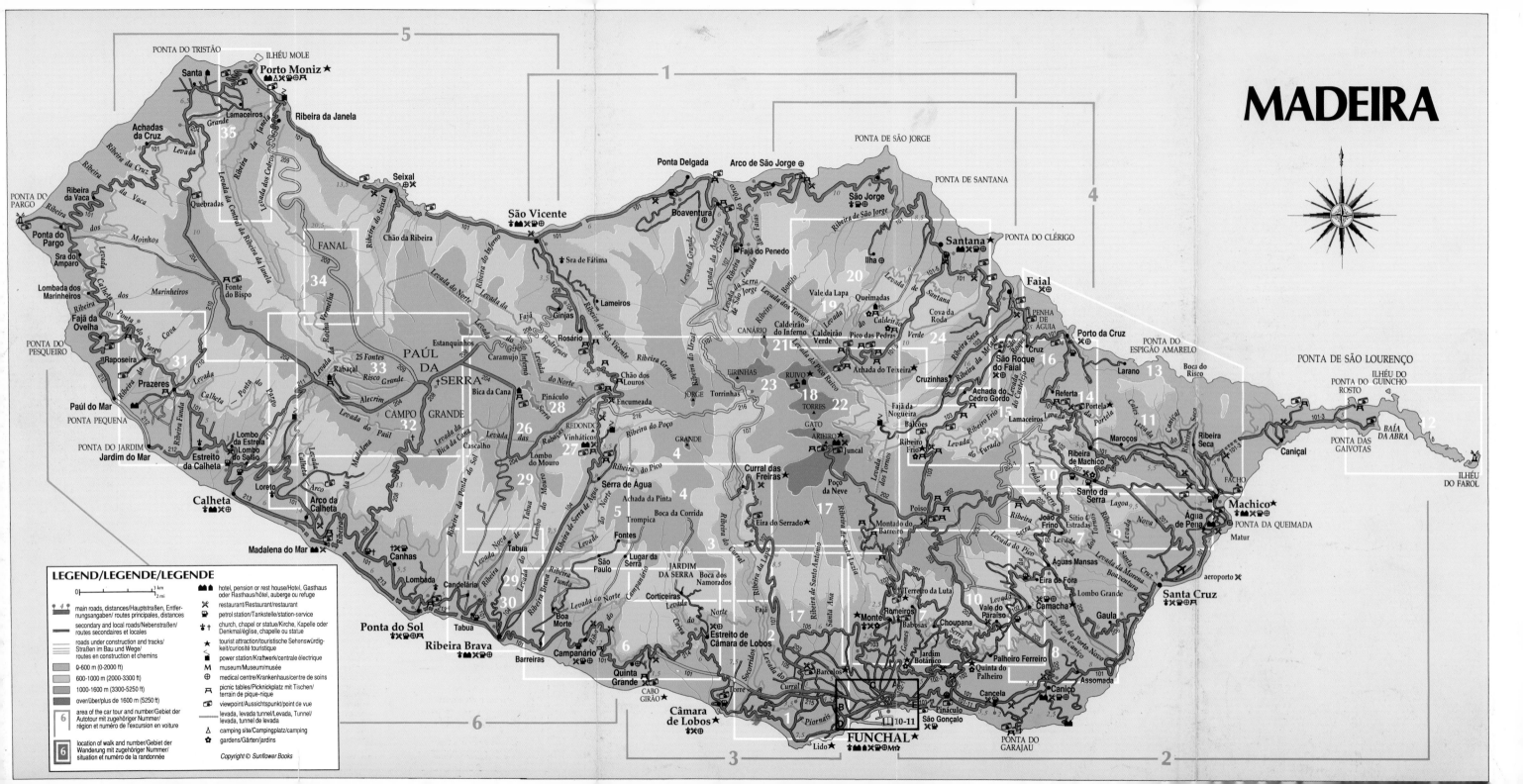

MADEIRA

LEGEND/LEGENDE/LEGENDE

0   1   2   3 km
0   1   2 mi

main roads, distances/Hauptstraßen, Entfernungsangaben/ routes principales, distances

secondary and local roads/Nebenstraßen/ routes secondaires et locales

roads under construction and tracks/ Straßen im Bau und Wege/ routes en construction et chemins

0-600 m (0-2000 ft)

600-1000 m (2000-3300 ft)

1000-1600 m (3300-5250 ft)

over/über/plus de 1600 m (5250 ft)

6 area of the car tour and number/Gebiet der Autotour mit zugehöriger Nummer/ région et numéro de l'excursion en voiture

6 location of walk and number/Gebiet der Wanderung mit zugehöriger Nummer/ situation et numéro de la randonnée

hotel, pension or rest house/Hotel, Gasthaus oder Rasthaus/hôtel, auberge ou refuge

restaurant/Restaurant/restaurant

petrol station/Tankstelle/station-service

church, chapel or statue/Kirche, Kapelle oder Denkmal/église, chapelle ou statue

tourist attraction/touristische Sehenswürdigkeit/curiosité touristique

power station/Kraftwerk/centrale électrique

museum/Museum/musée

medical centre/Krankenhaus/centre de soins

picnic tables/Picknickplatz mit Tischen/ terrain de pique-nique

viewpoint/Aussichtspunkt/point de vue

levada, levada tunnel/Levada, Tunnel/ levada, tunnel de levada

camping site/Campingplatz/camping

gardens/Gärten/jardins

Copyright © Sunflower Books

Girão, enjoy the splendid views of the coast above Caldeira (its chapel doesn't count as a church). Just before you go through the Cabo Girão tunnel at Cruz da Caldeira (**1h55min**), those prone to vertigo might feel a bit queasy, as the first sheer drops are encountered. It only takes three minutes to walk through this tunnel and it *can* be managed without a torch, since the path is very wide and the roof is high. Now Cabo Girão has disappeared, and you're in the valley of the Quinta Grande River. At **2h10min** the levada skirts the river bridge below the EN101. Climb right up a dirt path here to reach and cross the main road, avoiding this vertiginous channel. (You join the levada here on the west side of the road for Short walk 2; deduct 2h10min from all times given below.)

At **2h20min** count the second church — at Quinta Grande — as you continue along another high and narrow stretch, parallel to the EN101. Soon come to a spot that's exceptionally lovely in the autumn: a riot of sugar cane and blackberries in a tangle below stately pillars of pine and sweet chestnut standing proud in iron-rich soil. The houses are festooned with dahlias and the aroma of wood fires is in the air. On roof-tops, marrow and beans almost strangle the charming chimney-pots. The forest is alive with pink belladonna lilies.

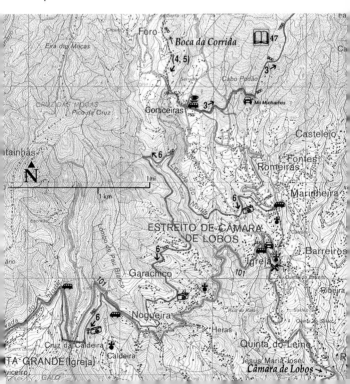

Count the church of Campanário off to the west and start heading up the valley of the Ribeira do Campanário, golden with broom in spring. Soon you'll pass a small eucalyptus plantation, before reaching (at **2h55min**) some more severe drops to the left. The path is often only about a metre wide (some 2ft), with scrub at the edge and then drops of about 70m/200ft. Keep your eyes fixed on the levada channel, for it will take one full minute to navigate this spot. You'll pass more paths down left and then see the EN101 above Campanário — the square-shaped U-turn is very easily recognised. At **3h20min** reach a lovely shady picnic spot, where the levada crosses the river. Here the

Outlook over the great cleft of the Ribeira Brava (Picnic 6)

Sure-footed walkers with a head for heights may like to know that the Levada do Norte continues north from Boa Morte to the power station at Serra de Água (dotted green lines on the map; 13km/8mi; 4h30min). We've walked this several times, and it is one of the most beautiful stretches of levada on the island, as you can see. But be warned: the channel is narrow and extremely vertiginous throughout, and there are no protective railings. Moreover, there are several long tunnels (torch required).

river sometimes rushes into the levada in a narrow concrete channel — a cooling sound on hot days.

Continue along through the wooded heights above Campanário and, in ten minutes (**3h30min**), you'll cross a dirt track. (If you're doing Short walk 2 and leaving the walk here, go straight down the track — do not take the left-hand fork. Descend gradually, first through a pine forest and later past many attractive houses, until you reach the EN101. Turn right at the main road to find the bus stop and an excellent local bar/shop.)

Those continuing on the levada will pass a cobbled trail beside a first water distribution centre and then reach a tarred road at **3h50min**. By **4h10min** a second water distribution centre is met in the Boa Morte pine forest. The *levadeiro* here has created a charming rose garden; he's very proud of it — so *do* tell him it's '**mween**-toh boh-**nee**-toh' (very pretty)! The setting is exceptionally beautiful (**P**6; photograph page 53), and the path is soft with pine needles. Just beyond the waterhouse you meet the asphalt road into the village (Short walk 3 comes in here).

After crossing the Boa Morte road, note the first dirt *track* off left, reached at about **4h20min**. For the moment pass it by and, in **4h40min**, look out over the great cleft of the Ribeira Brava (**P**6), its terraces, poplars, and banana plantations. The views north and south are magnificent. This levada flows from far, far north of your present viewpoint — see caption above and Walk 26.

Now return to the track first passed at about 4h20min and descend to Boa Morte (**5h10min**). It's unlikely you will be in time to catch the last bus of the day, so carry on down to the EN101 at Barreiras (**6h**). The bus stop is two minutes downhill right, by the sea — at the KM172 marker.

7 LEVADA DOS TORNOS: ROMEIROS • PALHEIRO FERREIRO • CAMACHA • LOMBO GRANDE • SITIO DAS QUATRO ESTRADAS

Map begins below and continues on pages 60-61.

Distance: 27.5km/17mi; 7h30min; but see Short walks below.

Grade, equipment, how to get there and return: see Short walks.

Short walks: This walk breaks conveniently into four stages —

1   Romeiros — Palheiro Ferreiro. 6km/3.7mi; 1h30min. Easy. Stout shoes, sunhat, picnic, water. Town 🚐 29 from Funchal to Romeiros; return from Palheiro Ferreiro to Funchal on 🚐 29 or 77 or town 🚐 37. Follow the notes beginning on page 61. Perhaps visit the Blandy Gardens (open 09.30-12.30 Mondays to Fridays, except holidays).

2   Palheiro Ferreiro — Camacha. 5.5km/3.4mi; 1h45min. Easy, but there is a very awkward tunnel to pass (10 minutes). Stout shoes, sunhat, picnic, water and a *good torch* for each member of the party. Town 🚐 37 or 🚐 29 or 77 from Funchal to Palheiro Ferreiro (ask for 'Levada dos Tornos'); return from Camacha to Funchal on 🚐 29 or 77. Notes begin on page 62.

3 Camacha — Lombo Grande. 6km/ 3.7mi; 1h30min. Easy, but sure-footedness and a head for heights required: the levada channel is very narrow in places. Blackberry thorns sometimes intrude, and you may have to walk *through* (seasonal) waterfalls. Equipment as for Short walk 2 above, plus extra cardigan, long trousers, anorak in cool weather, and whistle. *Don't forget the torches!* 🚌29 or 77 from Funchal to Camacha; return from Lombo Grande to Funchal on 🚌 60, or walk 0.6km uphill to Águas Mansas for 🚌 77. Notes page 63.

4 Lombo Grande — Sitio das Quatro Estradas. 11.5km/7.1mi; under 3h. Grade and equipment as for Short walk 3 (with a tiring 150m/500ft climb to the Sitio das Quatro Estradas). 🚌60 from Funchal (Boqueirão bus; ask for 'Levada dos Tornos, Lombo Grande'). From the bus stop, walk north up the EN206 for one minute to the levada. Or 🚌 77 to Águas Mansas, then walk 0.6km downhill to the levada. Notes page 65.

Alternative walks: You could join Walk 8, 9, or 10. You shouldn't have any difficulty, either, reversing Short walks 1, 2 or 3 (route-finding on Short walk 4, however, would be very difficult in reverse). Remember that dotted green lines on the map indicate routes that we have used and can recommend (although they may not be described in the book).

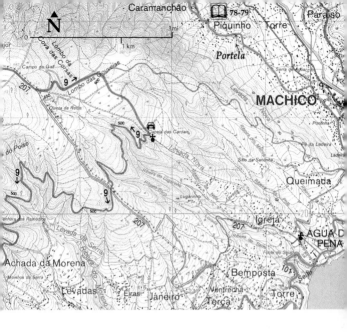

The pull-out touring map gives you a good overview of the Levada dos Tornos. Inaugurated in 1966, it is Madeira's most important levada, with 106km (66mi) of main channels. Water collected from three chief sources in the north flows to the power station at Fajã da Nogueira. (If you're sure-footed and tunnels don't worry you, you can explore the northern reaches of the Tornos on Walks 21 and 22.)

From the power station at Fajã da Nogueira (Walk 22) the levada flows through a very long tunnel (there are 16km/10mi of tunnels on the Tornos!) to the south of the island. It emerges into the open in the upper reaches of the João Gomes Valley, north of Romeiros, and then meanders on to irrigate more than 100,000 outlets between Funchal and Santa Cruz. And it is this southern run of the Tornos that we describe below*. From a height of 600 metres (almost 2000 feet) the hustle and bustle of life at sea level seems very far away; walking this levada path is like overflying the south coast in a balloon.

Start Short walk 1 at the end of the bus route in Romeiros. Climb steps and then the cobbled path on the right-hand side of the cul-de-sac. The path curves right in

*Actually we start about 1km southeast of the João Gomes Valley. *Experts, with no fear of unprotected precipices*, could have a look at the levada northwest of here, before it disappears into the tunnel (30min each way): climb steps at the right of the shop with the flagpole in Romeiros, then turn left on the levada (at first it is covered by concrete).

front of a house and then to the left; don't curve left, but turn right up the two short flights of concrete steps with iron railings. (If you come to a building with a flagpole, you have gone too far; note, too, if you are doing the walk in reverse: you must descend from the levada *before* this building with a flagpole.) At the top of the steps, you are on the levada, but it is covered by concrete. Turn right and continue to the end of the village on this covered walkway; you'll soon see the levada in full flow.

Follow the levada through groves of pine and mimosa and, in **35min**, you'll cross a cobbled road. Go through the gate opposite. A delightful chapel is on your right. This is the Quinta do Pomar. The levada channel runs behind the *quinta* and is too narrow to walk on. Take the path up to the left of the levada, to skirt the house itself.

In under **1h05min** you cross the EN201. In **1h30min** you cross the EN102 at the Levada dos Tornos bus stop (no '*paragem*' sign) above Palheiro Ferreiro; Short walk 1 ends here. The Blandy Gardens (and another bus stop) are ten minutes downhill, opposite the EN201. Continuing on the levada, cross the road into the setting shown below.

Short walk 2 begins at the Levada dos Tornos bus stop (no '*paragem*' sign). The levada is just by the stop. Head east into the setting shown below, with its bright flowers and ochre-red soil. Almost at once you overlook Palheiro Ferreiro, the south coast, and the Deserta Islands. In five minutes you pass a school on your right. Walk to the left of another large building; soon a stadium is above you, on the left. Cross a road and rejoin the levada by turning *sharp* left.

Here and above right: sun and shade on the Levada dos Tornos

In **20min** you come to a tunnel. *Watch your head!* A long stick helps, too, because the path is very narrow. (The path to the right of the tunnel would take you uphill and out of your way, and you would have a very slippery descent back to the levada. This route is shown by dotted green lines on the map, but we recommend going through the tunnel.) You emerge from this awkward tunnel in ten minutes, soon coming to various pleasant pine groves.

After leaving Nogueira's pretty valley (the Ribeira do Caniço), you reach an impassable tunnel (**1h**) by a small water distribution house. To its right, a fast-flowing levada courses south; to its left a steep dirt path leads up the wooded hillside to a tall building and a housing estate. Climb up, making for the buildings, and then bear right at the first crossroads. Keep straight on through the housing estate, until you come to the Caniço road (EN205). Turn left here but, one minute uphill, go right on a cobbled road into charming Ribeirinha. Pass a large house on your right with the inscription 'Levada dos Tornos' (**1h15min**) and keep straight on. Beyond the village shop (on the right; **1h20min**)*, continue northeast up this cobbled track to Camacha, keeping left at both forks you encounter. The 20-minute climb affords fine views down to the right over the Porto Novo Valley. You reach Camacha by the village square, the Achada da Camacha (**1h40min**).

Start Short walk 3 at the Café Relógio in the Achada da Camacha. Descend the road at the right of the café (the bank is on your right). Bear left downhill at a first fork, in

*To continue on the levada, leave the track just beyond this shop: a white arrow signpost (half hidden in greenery) directs you to the right. At a fork, bear right again. You rejoin the levada in under five minutes: pick up the notes on page 64, second paragraph; adjust times accordingly.

under a minute. (A housing estate is being built here; more forks may ensue; keep downhill.) In **7min** fork right at the crossroads (but look left for a fine view over the Porto Novo). A few minutes later, fork left down a cobbled track. In under **15min** you cross the levada; join it and turn left.

Having passed a house with a large palm tree (**23min**), you come to a short tunnel (**40min**). Beyond this tunnel (3min to pass), there is a possibility of vertigo for, although the levada path is very adequate, there are no railings, and the drops are severe — perhaps 50m/150ft. Often waterfalls cascade onto the path as well, and you may get soaked, for you must walk slowly and carefully. Watch out, too, for the concrete blocks in the path, supporting the pipe carrying some of the levada water. Still, we hope that some of you will manage this part of the walk in the lower part of the Porto Novo Valley (see also Walk 8), because it is one of the most beautiful stretches of the Tornos. Heading north from Camacha, you emerge from another short tunnel and, suddenly, birds and cascades are singing everywhere. By **50min** you come to the pools at the head of the valley, where a waterfall crashes into the river; all else is stillness. Eight minutes later you pass a dyke on the right and enjoy the views of the valley shown below.

Picnic 7a. From the tunnel with windows you overlook the great bowl of terracing in the Porto Novo Valley. This grassy 'amphitheatre' of cultivation is best seen in spring, when golden broom cloaks the hillsides.

Pass through the third and shortest tunnel (**1h**), before skirting round a tunnel with 'windows' at about **1h10min** (be sure to climb up steps beyond this tunnel to rejoin the Tornos; the levada continuing ahead runs down to Gaula). Take a break anywhere along here (**P**7a), before you lose the views shown opposite — but only picnic on uncultivated land! Across the valley you can see Salgados, dribbling down the ridge (Walk 8). All too soon, you reach a water catchment at Lombo Grande. Just beyond it is the EN206 (**1h30min**). Turn right and descend for under a minute to the bus stop, if you are leaving the walk here.

Short walk 4 begins where the levada crosses the EN206 at Lombo Grande. Head east and, in under **10min** you have good views over the airport and São Lourenço. After **20min** you pass through a very short tunnel (no torch needed) and come out in the Boaventura Valley (**P**7b). While the Porto Novo is our favourite part of the Tornos in spring, in summer the Boaventura Valley takes the prize. The terraces are golden with wheat, and the levada paths are aglow with blue and white agapanthus — so tall and thick that they are almost like hedgerows. By **50min** you reach the head of a deep tributary, the Vinháticos. Five minutes later a promontory to your right is a superb picnic spot. In **1h15min** you cross a cobbled trail. Two further trails are crossed in the next 15 minutes; beyond the third one (**1h30min**) you are in a new valley — the Santa Cruz.

Cross a cobbled road in **1h50min** and then a very *wide* cobbled path (**2h05min**). Ten minutes later (**2h15min**) watch for a *narrow* path down on your right and the narrow cobbled steps opposite it, on your left. In **2h20min** the levada ends. Unbelievable! How can this magnificent watercourse, which has carried you through the most beautiful valleys in the southeast, have abandoned you without warning? Its waters shoot out into a tank some 200m/650ft below, to feed the Levada Nova (see Walk 9). A pipe coming in from the Levada da Serra (Walk 10) runs down and over to the reservoir at Santo da Serra.

Return to the path passed in 2h15min and climb it for a couple of minutes. You emerge in fields, where electricity wires cross in front of you. Head towards them, keeping to the left of the plots. At a stone wall, bear left. Bear left again at a second wall, immediately coming to a cobbled track. Go left uphill, passing a walkway on the left. Go straight over at a crossroads, always climbing. You reach the EN102 at the Sitio das Quatro Estradas (**2h55min**). Wait for the bus opposite the Poiso road (no '*paragem*' sign).

8 CAMACHA • LEVADA DO CANIÇO • ASSOMADA

Map page 60; photograph page 28   Distance: 6km/3.8mi; 2h20min

Grade: moderate, with a *very* steep — sometimes slippery — descent of 250m/820ft to the levada. Surefootedness is essential; **possibility of vertigo** on the levada.

Equipment: walking boots, long trousers, sunhat, picnic, water; extra cardigan and anorak in cool weather

How to get there: 🚌 29 or 77 from Funchal to Camacha
To return: 🚌 2 (or one of many others) from Assomada to Funchal

Short walk: Assomada — Porto Novo Valley — Assomada. See notes for Picnic 8, page 13.

Alternative walk: Camacha — Levada dos Tornos. A path from the Levada do Caniço drops to the river, from where a *very overgrown* path climbs to the Tornos (Walk 7); see dotted green lines on the map.

Any season, any time of day, is suitable for this splendid walk in one of Madeira's most lush valleys. And this is a less vertiginous way to see the lower Porto Novo Valley than by following Walk 7; although the drops on this walk are quite severe, they are not as *sheer,* since there is generally scrub at the edge of the levada path.

Start the walk at the 'Centro de Saúde' in the southeast corner of the square (to the left of the café with the clock). Take the steep cobbled track heading south, at the left of this medical centre. In ten minutes you come to the school, where the track forks. Here go left on the lily-bordered cobbled path. It descends very steeply into the delightful 'perched' hamlet of Salgados, hidden in apple trees and decorated from top to toe with willow.

Keep on the same path, passing a tap on the right. Following the electricity wires, slither down stone 'steps', which drop you abruptly onto the Levada do Caniço (**35min**). Turn right to ramble to Assomada. Almost at once, you will see a path down left to a bridge over the river, from where you could climb to the Tornos Levada.

A particularly lovely promontory (*P*8; see photograph page 28) is met in **1h40min**, just beyond a grove of golden broom and a short tunnel. Here you can picnic nestled in sugar cane, poppies and thistles — while you look out over the valley, the south coast and the Deserta Islands.

In well under **2h**, a concrete path crosses, just before a house. Turn down left, with a raised water channel on your left, to reach a road in half a minute. Turn left and follow the road downhill, past an electricity substation on your right. Walk behind Assomada's church (**2h20min**) and, on meeting the main road, bear left. The bus stop is just here, in the lay-by on the east side of the church.

9 SANTO DA SERRA • LEVADA NOVA • SITIO DAS QUATRO ESTRADAS

Map pages 60-61; photograph page 22

Distance: 14km/8.7mi; 4h10min

Grade: easy-moderate, with a steep climb of 250m/820ft at the end of the walk. Following the levada, you need to be sure-footed and have a head for heights (**possibility of vertigo**).

Equipment: stout shoes (walking boots preferable), long trousers, sunhat, picnic, water; extra cardigan and anorak in cool weather

How to get there: 🚌 20, 25, 77 or 78 from Funchal to Santo da Serra. If you object to walking along tarmac for an hour, take a taxi from there to the Capela dos Cardais, where the levada walk starts (deduct 50min).
To return: 🚌 77 from the Sitio das Quatro Estradas to Funchal

Special note: We strongly recommend that you do the walk in the direction described. Trying to descend to the levada from the Sitio das Quatro Estradas is difficult — the path is hard to find and, once you are on it, the descent is very steep and slippery.

I f you've walked the Levada dos Tornos from start to finish, wouldn't you think that you'd seen the best of the Santa Cruz Valley? After all, the Tornos is 100m/330ft higher than the Levada Nova. Wouldn't you expect it to be greener, more vertiginous, more beautiful and more exciting than this lower levada? You are in for a surprise!

Start out at Santo da Serra's church. Follow the road (EN207) southeast, towards the golf course. Pass by the park on your left, and the road adjacent to it, and continue straight on to a Y-fork in front of the Quinta da Paz (**15min**). Bear left here, to pass the golf course on your left and the *lagoa* (reservoir) on the conical hill above right. Beyond the clubhouse for the golf course, you reach another fork. Go left and continue for about eight minutes, to another fork, where you go right. Ten minutes' descent brings you the little Capela dos Cardais, on your right (**50min**), by a noisy and refreshing water distribution point.

The Levada Nova lies just above and behind the chapel; join it and head west. The way is graced by *Senecio* and passion flowers, but some blackberry thorns tear at your long trousers too. Cross a grassy track in **1h20min** and then the EN207 running south to the airport (**1h28min**). Three minutes later, beyond an unmade track, you come to the long buildings of a piggery. A couple of stone-laid trails cross your way not far beyond here.

Having rounded the Ribeira do Moreno, in **2h30min** you meet a road with electricity poles, by a waterhouse. It leads uphill to Santo da Serra and would be a less steep ascent that our suggested route, *but* you would miss the best part of the walk! Cross the road; a water tank is on your right. The levada is appreciably wider now, as you head up into the Ribeira de Santa Cruz. This stretch of the Levada Nova, on the eastern side of the Santa Cruz Valley, is guaranteed to delight even the most jaded levada-walker. Masses upon masses of blue and white agapanthus dance along the curves of the channel, a waterfall bursts upon the scene — even in mid-summer — and then, in **3h10min**, you come to an incredible emerald-green fern-covered grotto. A niche in the muddy banks reveals a nest, with two gawping baby birds taking you for their parents. But there is more to come: just round the bend, a solitary house on the right is drenched in fuchsias, which grow wild in another glen. River pools shimmer down to the left. It's all to wonderful to last, and it doesn't. Almost at once the source of the levada is met at a water catchment, where overspill water pours in from the Levada dos Tornos above. A pipe (some of it underground) carries water here from the Levada da Serra (Walk 10) as well. Another pipe, this one visible, runs up to the *lagoa* above Santo da Serra.

From the water catchment, return to a path on your right, just two minutes along. It takes you down to a bridge over the river pools. Relax at this delightful fuchsia glen with its gurgling pools (illustrated on page 22), before heading back to Santo da Serra's highlands. Then climb the path on the other side of the bridge. At a fork met almost immediately, go left. You reach the Levada dos Tornos in 15 minutes. Turn left on it (or first go right for a few minutes, to follow it to where it ends and spills over into the catchment you've just left). A few minutes to the left of where your path came up onto the Tornos, you meet a crossing path. Climb up to the right for a couple of minutes. You emerge in fields, where electricity wires cross in front of you. From here use in the notes in the last paragraph on page 65, to reach the Sitio das Quatro Estradas about 30 minutes from the Tornos (**4h10min**).

10 LEVADA DA SERRA: CHOUPANA •
CAMACHA • PORTELA

Map begins on pages 58-59, continues on pages 60-61, and ends on page 79; photograph page 27.

Distance: See introduction and 'The entire length' below.

Grade: easy throughout, but there is always an initial climb to levada level. (In some cases you can reach the levada by car, if a friend is willing to play taxi: look for the 🚐 symbol on the map.)

Equipment: stout shoes, sunhat, picnic, water; extra cardigans and anorak in cool weather (especially for the stretch north of Camacha)

How to get there and return: See Short walks 1-5 below.

Short walks: See 1-5 below (all are easy).

The Levada da Serra was our first experience of walking on Madeira, and it may well be yours — especially if you book an 'organised' levada walk. Since much of the way is now signposted, and there is little chance of getting lost, we don't describe the walk in detail. Instead, we are responding to users' requests for more information about joining the walk at convenient points and doing these segments in reverse.

Don't expect to find much water in this levada — most of it has been diverted to the Tornos, some 200m/650ft below (Walk 7). Enjoy instead the flora (azaleas, hydrangeas, gorse, lilies, rhododendrons — depending on the season) and the pleasant shade of eucalyptus and oak trees. *Do* expect to meet coachloads of walkers...

This levada is some 27km/17mi long, from the Lamaceiros waterhouse above Portela to its end at Choupana, southeast of Romeiros. It can be done in one fell swoop, but it breaks conveniently into five short walks.

The entire length: Choupana — Lamaceiros — Portela. 30km/18.6mi; 8h. Grade: moderate (on account of the length). Take a 🚐 taxi from Funchal (ask for 'Levada da Serra, Choupana'). You will be dropped off on the EN201, by a steep cobbled track. Climb this for under eight minutes, until you find a short cobbled path on the right. This leads to the (dry) levada, which is hidden by tall grass and difficult to see. Follow the levada all the way to the Lamaceiros waterhouse, then pick up the notes for Walk 25 to descend to Portela on the Levada da Portela for 🚌 20, 53 or 78. Alternatively, leave at the Santo da Serra waterhouse: descend the track on the south side of this waterhouse to the EN102, then walk on to Santo da Serra for 🚌 20, 25, 77 or 78 (a somewhat shorter walk of 27km/16.8mi; under 8h). If you do the walk in reverse (see Short walk 5 below, 'To begin at Portela'), remember that there is no transport at Choupana; but see notes for Short walk 1 in reverse. *Note:* The levada is covered by a road in the Porto Novo Valley; the short walks omit this stretch.

Short walks

1 Choupana — Paradise Valley. 4km/2.5mi; 1h05min. Access as 'The entire length'. On reaching the EN203 to Poiso, just beyond the *quinta* at Paradise Valley, turn down right to the EN102. Here you can pick up 🚌 29 or 77. To walk this stretch in reverse, join the levada as in Short

walk 2; turn left and walk to Choupana. There is no transport here. When the levada ends, turn left down the steep cobbled trail to the crossing of the EN201 (6min). Go straight over and descend for about 15min, to find the Levada dos Tornos running under the road. Turn right on this levada and follow it to Romeiros. Leave the levada just before the building with a flagpole. Two flights of concrete steps, on your left, take you down to the road, where you can catch town 🚌 29 to Funchal.

2 Paradise Valley — Camacha. 6km/3.7mi; 1h40min. Take 🚌 29 or 77 from Funchal to 'Vale Paraíso' (pronounced '**Val** Pah-rah-**ee**-soh'). Climb the EN203 for 20min to the levada crossing. Turn right. Ignore any forks running down to the right until you come to a crossroads at a group of buildings (after about 1h10min on the levada). Signposting here, on your left, indicates Choupana (the way you've come) and Santo da Serra (straight on). Bear right downhill. Immediately you will see a sign for Camacha (🚌29, 77), on the building on your right. To do this stretch in reverse, climb the cobbled road behind Camacha's church (where the EN102 forks right to Santo da Serra). Fork left 200m/yds beyond the gates of the Quinta das Almas. At the levada crossing (under 15min), a signpost indicates 'Choupana'). At the crossing of the EN203 to Poiso, turn down left to the EN102, where you can pick up 🚌 29 or 77 to Funchal. Or carry on to Choupana; for transport from there, see Short walk 1.

3 Águas Mansas — Sítio das Quatro Estradas. 12km/7.4mi; 3h15min. Take 🚌 77 from Funchal to Águas Mansas, or 🚌 60 from Funchal to Boqueirão (from where you must walk 0.6km uphill to the EN102; add 10min). From the joining of the EN206 and the EN102, walk 100m/yds towards Santo da Serra, then turn left up a track. You reach the levada in about 10min. Turn right and follow it (**P**10) as far as the EN202 to Poiso; there turn down right to the EN102 to catch 🚌 77 at the Sítio das Quatro Estradas ('place where four roads join'). To join the levada from the Sítio das Quatro Estradas, see Short walk 4. Your descent to Águas Mansas comes up after just before the crossing of the noisy Levada do Pico. *Note:* We do not recommend starting this Short walk at Camacha, because the levada is covered by a road in the Porto Novo Valley.

4 Sítio das Quatro Estradas — Santo da Serra. 8km/5mi; 2h. Take 🚌 77 from Funchal to the Sítio das Quatro Estradas (pronounced '**See**-tee-oh dahs **Kwa**-troh Esh-**trah**-dahsh'). Climb the EN202 to Poiso for under 15 minutes and turn right at the crossing of the levada. About 1h15min later, you cross a track and come to a waterhouse. Enjoy its charming gardens, then return to the track* and descend to the EN102 (25min). Wait for 🚌 77 there, or walk downhill and turn left into Santo da Serra (20min), to catch 🚌 20, 77 or 78. To do this stretch in reverse, join the levada as in Short walk 5. On reaching the crossing of the EN202 to Poiso, turn down left to the EN102, where you can catch 🚌 77.

5 Santo da Serra — Portela. 7.5km/4.7mi; 2h15min. Take 🚌 20, 25, 77 or 78 from Funchal to Santo da Serra, but get off at the turn-off into Santo da Serra (EN207); do not go into the village. Climb the EN102 to a track* on the left (6-7min uphill) and follow it up to the Santo da Serra waterhouse. Turn right and walk to the next waterhouse (Lamaceiros). From here use the notes on page 106 and map on page 105 (Walk 25), to go to Portela. To begin at Portela, walk down the EN102 (signposted to Funchal) for a couple of minutes. You pass a path on your right leading to a shrine; beyond this path, steps on the right take you up to the levada (a climb of 200m/650ft). You are following the end of Walk 25, in reverse.

---

*This rough track is shown on the military maps reproduced in this book as a road, but it has never been surfaced.

11 LEVADA DO CANIÇAL: MAROÇOS •
CANIÇAL TUNNEL • PICO DO FACHO

Map pages 78-79; photograph page 23

Distance: 14km/8.7mi; 4h20min

Grade: easy

Equipment: stout shoes, sunhat, long-sleeved shirt, picnic, water; extra cardigan and anorak in cool weather

How to get there: 🚌156 from Funchal to Maroços
To return: 🚌113 from the Pico do Facho bus stop to Funchal

Short walks: Both are easy and both start by the Pico do Facho bus stop at the Caniçal tunnel (access via 🚌113 from Funchal or Machico). Equipment as above.
1 Caniçal tunnel — Boca do Risco — Ribeira Seca. 8.5km/5.3mi; 2h10min. Join the Levada do Caniçal by the waterhouse on the north side of the road and head west. After 40min, you meet the path to Boca do Risco: here stone steps cross the levada; they lead up from a house (and electricity pole). Follow the path up to the right; it's a 30min climb from here to Boca do Risco (photograph and notes pages 76, 77; Walk 13). Return the same way and then descend past the house, following the electricity poles down to the road in the valley. Follow it south to the EN101-3 at Ribeira Seca. Return to Machico or Funchal on 🚌113.
2 Caniçal tunnel—Pico do Facho—Caniçal tunnel. 2.5km/1.6mi; 1h. The road to the peak is by the bus stop. Access/return by 🚌113.

The 'mimosa levada' offers an entrancing and easy walk, well within the reach of most visitors to Madeira. If you like, you can extend the walk by including a (50min return) detour to Boca do Risco. Or you can shorten the walk by leaving out the climb to Pico do Facho.

The walk begins in Maroços (the end of the 156 bus route, where a road is under construction to Ribeira de Machico and Portela). Two garages are facing you, and a footbridge runs between them. Cross the bridge and climb the 100 concrete steps beyond it, to reach the levada. Turn *left* at first, along the road beside the levada. Pass an old mill and a newer building on the left and then, round a corner, in **5min** come to a glen of willow and lilies. Here you'll find the old mill shown on page 23 standing guard at the source of the island's first 'new' levada (16km/10mi long; 1949). This area is known as Fonte Vermelha ('the

Red Spring'; *P*11), named for the reddish-coloured porous rock through which the water filters. Note the fine basalt prisms behind the mill, formed when the molten lava solidified. Go under the raised mill-race behind the mill and down to the river — an idyllic picnic spot.

Now return the way you came and follow the flow of the levada through some enchanting valleys. You'll quickly gain the narrow Ribeira das Cales, a first glimpse of the gentle landscapes that make this walk such a delight. Past the eastern end of Maroços, come into the valley of the Ribeira Grande. There is little habitation from here until almost the end of the walk, but the handiwork of the Madeiran farmer is all around. *Palheiros* dot the landscape, mere specks of red and white in the great bowls of greenery. Perhaps you will meet a youngster bringing home a melon for dinner — he puts it into the levada and 'steers' his melon-boat with a stick… But it is more likely that your only companions will be full-throated frogs singing to their hearts' content.

A short tunnel is met at the end of this valley (**1h55min**; no torch needed) and then two waterhouses perched up beside the levada. Twenty minutes past the second one, there is a good route down to Ribeira Seca if you're pressed for time — just follow the electricity poles. The main walk continues by delving into the Ribeira da Noia, where it becomes obvious why we call this the 'mimosa levada'! All year round these golden trees will frame your photographs of the unforgettable valleys. The great cornucopia of the valley of the Ribeira Seca is reached all too soon. Linger a while beneath some oaks; there's a feast for the eyes all round you, and your walk through the valleys is drawing to an end. From here you can see bright Machico and the Deserta Islands glimmering in the sun.

At about **2h40min**, soon after passing a narrow U-bend in the levada, you will notice stone steps crossing the channel. They come up from a house and electricity pole. This path leads north to Boca do Risco (50min return; photograph and notes pages 76, 77; Walk 13). You'll reach the Caniçal tunnel in just over **3h20min**, and you may wish to end the walk here and catch an earlier bus (the levada continues through the tunnel and on to Caniçal). If you have time, we'd suggest a visit to Pico do Facho; the asphalt road is just opposite the levada waterhouse at the tunnel. The views over Machico Bay and São Lourenço Point from this easily-climbed peak are glorious in late afternoon. You return to the EN101 in **4h20min**.

12 PONTA DE SÃO LOURENÇO

Distance: 7km/4.3mi; 3h

Grade: expert; only recommended for sure-footed walkers with a head for heights; **danger of vertigo!**

Equipment: walking boots, long trousers, long-sleeved shirt, sunhat, picnic, water, whistle; cardigans and anorak with hood in cool weather

How to get there and return: 🚌 113 to from Funchal to Caniçal and from there a taxi to the viewpoint at Abra Bay, or by 🚗 : park at Abra Bay, where the EN101-3 ends (Car tour 2).

Short walk: Abra Bay viewpoint — lookouts over the north coast and the tip of the island. Easy; 35 minutes return; *especially recommended* as a leg-stretcher on Car tour 2. Stout shoes, sunhat. Access as main walk. Follow the main walk for 20min; then return to the car park.

The sun-tanned arm of São Lourenço Point beckons you when you first approach the island by air. Whether you're an expert walker or just a novice, *do* spend a day out here. Not only are there interesting flora and rock strata to be seen, but you come almost face-to-face with the full fury of the Atlantic thrashing against the coast and the offshore rocks. Wear your sunglasses! The colours of the sea and the rocks are dazzling.

Palm trees shade the lone house on São Lourenço Point, framing your view of Abra Bay and the straits.

Start the walk where the EN101-3 ends, at tranquil Abra Bay (**P**12). Go forward on the track straight off the viewpoint, between iron posts. It peters out into a path and, in **15min**, you come to a fork: bear left and quickly come to one of the island's most breath-taking viewpoints over the north coast (**P**12). You'll be able to see the headlands as far west as São Jorge, but what is most astounding is the colour and shape of the rock formations below you: the lava rock seems almost fluorescent, so intense is its purple-red colour as it thrusts up from the emerald sea.

From here follow follow the path heading south and slightly east. Make for the telephone pole; some splodges of red paint guide you over the bedrock. The path *appears* to end at this pole (**20min**), from where you will have exceptionally fine views of the lighthouse at the end of the point, the eyelet in the lighthouse rock, and the Deserta Islands. Those of you doing the Short walk should return from this point to the car parking area.

Those continuing the walk may well wonder what to do next. The keen eye will spot a splodge of red paint on a rock, waymarking an ongoing path, over bedrock. We started to follow this, but found that it was too treacherous for our liking and that it was taking us too far downhill (although we *did* have particularly good views of some volcanic chimneys after about five minutes of descent). Instead of following the red paint waymark, we suggest that you turn *sharp left* from the pole and climb up the 'nose' of bedrock. Once you are halfway up this small

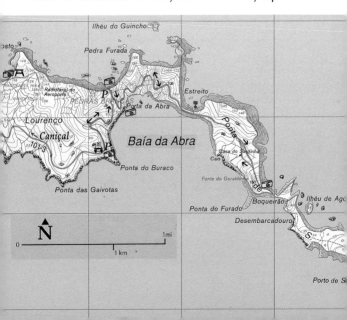

peak, you will see a narrow path leading northeast, out to the point. The way is still mostly over bedrock, but it *is* discernible. (You will also spot a path to the beach.)

Some **45min** into the hike the character of the walk has changed completely, and you might like to take a break in a softly-carpeted field of wild oats and barley, sprinkled with thistles. Ten minutes later (**55min**) come to another telephone pole. There's a stone marker here, too, 'TC/75'. The worst part of the walk awaits you now — a very narrow descent beside an escarpment. It's particularly difficult for the short of leg to find footholds, especially when contemplating the foaming jaws of death below. Fortunately this only lasts half a minute, although to Pat it seems an hour and knowing that she has to return the same way *almost* ruins the rest of the walk.

But from here on the going is really easy and totally exhilarating. Beyond a flourish of ice plants (*Mesembryanthemum crystallinum*), the path passes to the left of an abandoned house. Continue up to the top of the hill beyond it (**1h35min**). The path ends here: the 'hill' you have climbed is only half a hill; beyond the summit there is simply … an abyss. You're at 150m — almost 500ft — a fantastic vantage point relative to the surrounding terrain. If you can bear to look over the edge into the 'nothingness', you'll see the rest of the peninsula hanging on by a 'thread' of rock, and the Ilhéu do Farol with its lighthouse; these shreds of land are only accessible from the sea.

It may have been a slog up the hill in full sun, but now

you have the joy of running down it, making for the lone house, a lovely picnicking spot in the shade of palms. It's so romantic, you might even be tempted to try Eve's trick and share an apple with your mate. The house was built in the early 1900s by a business man from Funchal called Sardinha; a little quay (*cais*) for his boat is nearby. From here return to your outgoing path (not far uphill from the house), go by the nasty place at the stone marker (**2h15min**) and back to the car park (**3h**).

13 NORTH COAST PATH: CANIÇAL TUNNEL • BOCA DO RISCO • PORTO DA CRUZ

Distance: 13.5km/8.4mi; 4h10min

Grade: expert; sure-footedness and a head for heights essential. Beyond Boca do Risco the north coast path is narrow, often slippery, and *sometimes impassable due to landslides;* unprotected drops of 350m/1150ft; **danger of vertigo!**

Equipment: walking boots, sunhat, long trousers, long-sleeved shirt, picnic, water, whistle, 2 cardigans, anorak with hood

How to get there: 🚌 113 from Funchal to the Pico do Facho bus stop on the west side of the Caniçal tunnel

To return: 🚌 53 or 78 from Porto da Cruz to Funchal

Short walk: see Short walk 11-1 on page 71.

Alternative walk: Larano — Espigão Amarelo — Porto da Cruz. 7.5km/ 4.7mi; 2h35min. Easy, but sure-footedness is essential, and you must have a head for heights (**possibility of vertigo**). Equipment as above. Access and return: 🚌 53 or 78 from Funchal to Porto da Cruz. Take a taxi from Porto da Cruz to Larano, where the tarred road ends. (🚗: You can also drive here and just take a short walk along the coastal path.) At Larano go straight ahead up a couple of concrete steps (two houses are *just beside* this path, on your right). Climb to the left of a cow house and then head east. In five minutes a levada appears on your left. Continue east beside it; this path takes you straight to the coastal path, 15min from Larano (ignore all paths heading up *sharp* left). Follow the north coast path for as long as you like, or until it becomes too vertiginous. (Or follow it all the way to Boca do Risco, from where you could join Walk 11.) To return to Porto da Cruz from Larano, pick up the notes for the main walk at the 3h05min-point. *NB: See also Alternative walk 14.*

T his is a walk of contrasts. Amble along the Levada do Caniçal, marvelling at the sun-blessed fertility of Madeira's soil. You can forget for a while what it has cost the islanders in toil, for there are few tiny terraces here, just lush farmland. Then climb from the levada to the crest of the north coast. Here the wind — often chill — wakes you

The north coast path from Boca do Risco, looking west; see also photograph page 31.

to the cruel realities of life on the island. The north coast between Boca do Risco and Porto da Cruz is perhaps the quintessence of Madeira — nowhere else on the island can match its rugged, proud beauty in sunlight; few places in the world could match its harsh anger when lashed by storms.

It is not wise to walk the coastal path in winter and, at *any time*, storm damage may cause landslides (generally between Boca do Risco and Espigão Amarelo, below Pico Larano), **making the walk impassable. Never be foolish enough to attempt to cross landslides here: one slip of the soil and you would plunge 350m/1150ft into the sea.**

Begin the walk at the Pico do Facho bus stop on the west side of the Caniçal tunnel. Cross the road and find the Levada do Caniçal (see Walk 11) behind the waterhouse. Follow the levada northwest for **40min**, until you come to stone steps crossing. They lead up from a house and electricity pole. Here bear right on an uphill path. The climb is gradual at first, through farmland, where you will likely as not see children carrying huge wicker baskets of fodder on their heads. Later brush and bilberry take over, leading to forests of mimosa and pine. The air is delicious and fresh, with just a hint of salt blowing in from the sea. Within **1h15min** you reach Boca do Risco (the 'dangerous pass') — the wonderful viewpoint shown opposite. Here are houseleeks like great cabbages, snowball trees, thistles, gorse, ferns, laurel, heath and wild flowers in every colour you can imagine. Off across the sea to the northeast, Porto Santo should be clearly visible.

Turn left to make for Porto da Cruz. In **2h** pass through a gate and soon, looking east, you will enjoy views of Ilhéu do Guincho ('Screech Islet') — so called because the wind shrieks through its tiny eyelet. This is one of our favourite views on Madeira … dazzling in morning sun or glimmering in afternoon glow. Then new headlands come into view and, by **2h30min**, you'll reach a promontory with a stone marker just above the Espigão Amarelo ('Sharp Yellow Point') … a splendid lunch spot.

Round one more headland before your first views of Porto da Cruz. Pass above Cova das Pedras, a semi-circular cove hardly visible from the cliffs. The character of the coastal path changes dramatically almost before you notice it, its starkness now softened by pine forests and, in the autumn, banks of pink belladonna lilies. You look down to a sea of palest turquoise through pine trees standing tall in ochre-red soil. The waves break over the rocks below again and again and again, creating endless patterns of the finest lace.

About five minutes past Cova das Pedras (**3h 05min**), the path leaves the cliff. Just 30m/yds past the narrow ridge between the sea and the valley, the way forks. Go right, with a narrow levada on your right. After about 6-7 minutes, when you see a cow house below you, take the path down left, to pass to the right of it. You reach an asphalt road in Larano (**3h20min**). Follow it downhill, through a valley with emerald crops and laden vines. In ten minutes, it bends sharply left. Straight ahead you'll see a hill with caves. Leave the road here, taking concrete steps down to the right. (Of course, you could follow the road all the way to Porto da Cruz.) You pass to the left of the caves on a stone-laid path which then takes you down to the sea. The mouth of the Ribeira da Maiata is crossed on a storm-damaged footbridge (**3h 45min**), and you climb up the far side, to a road. Turn right and enjoy the fine view of Porto da Cruz, focusing on its rock, old sugar refinery and church. The road takes you into the centre (**4h10min**). The bus stops in front of the Centro de Saúde (no *'paragem'* sign).

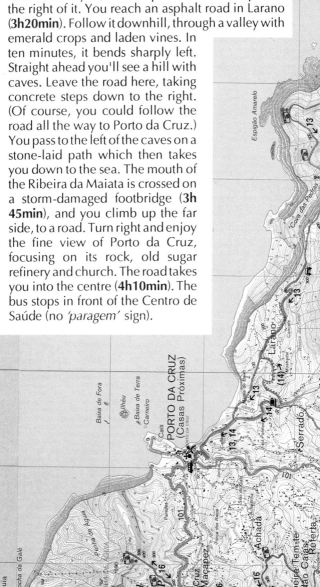

14 PORTELA • CRUZ DA GUARDA • PORTO DA CRUZ

Map pages 78-79　　　　　　　　**Distance:** 6km/3.7mi; 1h55min

Grade: moderate, with a very steep descent. You must be sure-footed.

Equipment: walking boots, long trousers, sunhat, picnic, water

How to get there: 🚌 20, 53 or 78 from Funchal to Portela
To return: 🚌 53 or 78 from Porto da Cruz to Funchal

Alternative walk: Portela — Larano — Espigão Amarelo — Porto da Cruz. 12.5km/7.8mi; 4h35min. Grade/access as above. At the Maiata road go right over the bridge, then left to Larano (2h), for Alternative walk 13.

In the 1800s the *borracheiros* used this trail to transport wine, carried in goatskins on their backs, from Porto da Cruz to the south. Visually stunning in its own right, this walk is an ideal approach to Alternative walk 13.

Begin on the tarred road on the north side of the 'Casa da Portela'; it soon reverts to track (***P***14). After 200m/yds, turn left down an old stone-laid path. Zigzag steeply down (slippery when wet), enjoying superb views of Porto da Cruz and other villages and hamlets on the northeast coast, all dwarfed by Penha de Águia. In **35min**, on the outskirts of Cruz da Guarda, the path forks. Go left, passing a water storage tank on your left, and meet a tarred road (**40min**). Follow it to the right for just a few metres/yards, then swing sharp left down a minor road. (This road soon crosses the Levada Nova, but various obstructions block the path between here and the start of Walk 16.) Continue down the steep road, through the strung-out village of Cruz da Guarda. The road peters out into a path, two rivers are crossed on a single bridge, and you reach the Maiata road (**1h25min**). Bear left into Porto da Cruz (**1h55min**).

15 CRUZ • LEVADA DO CASTELEJO • CRUZ

Map pages 78-79, then 105   **Distance:** 9km/5.6mi; 2h50min

Grade: easy, but sure-footedness and a head for heights essential; **danger of vertigo** on one very short stretch (*no* protective railings).

Equipment: walking boots, long trousers, sunhat, picnic, water

How to get there and return: 🚌 53 or 78 from Funchal to Cruz and back, or 🚗: park at the tiny electricity substation at Cruz (just east of Faial), or as close to it as you can, without blocking the (busy) EN101.

Alternative walk: Referta — Levada do Castelejo — Cruz — (Penha de Águia). Follow Walk 16 for 50min (easy), then do this walk (3h30min in all). Or go on to climb Penha de Águia (expert; 5h30min in all).

U tter bliss! A fast-flowing levada, still totally unspoilt by parties of walkers ... with river pools that have never seen a plastic carrier bag or sardine tin. So far. In just over an hour you move from the cornucopia of cultivation below Penha de Águia into the wilderness of the Ribeiro Frio, with its mimosas and ancient fine-leaved laurels.

Start the walk by the sign for Cruz. A few paces uphill from the tiny electricity substation (almost opposite the 'Cruz' sign) there are two roads: Climb the old one, on the right, passing a bar/shop on your right immediately. Ignore a road off to the right in five minutes, and keep ahead uphill on cobbles. Within **10min** you come to the levada on your right (Walk 16 comes in here, from the left). Turn right on the fast-flowing levada, walking against the current. Chartreuse-coloured vines will frame your photographs of Penha de Águia, São Roque and Faial.

Beyond a road crossing, in **20min**, São Roque's church on the next *lombo* seems close enough to touch. Then you turn sharp left up the magnificent valley of the Ribeira de São Roque (*P*15), almost at once passing under a water-

fall. In **40min** the levada channel is but a ribbon on the escarpment, and *there is no protection from the sheer drops.* Other drops are encountered further on, but they are all edged by trees or scrub, and the path is always at least 60cm/2ft wide.

In **1h25min** you're at the levada's source; stone steps take you down to the boulder-strewn Ribeiro Frio. The setting is magnificent. The river pools are so clear that you might be tempted to swim. Only birdsong disturbs the peace of this primaeval place.

From here return to Cruz (**2h50min**).

Penha de Águia ('Eagle Rock'), the great landmark of the north (Picnic 16; Walks 13-16, 25; Car tours 1 and 4). This photograph was taken on Walk 14.

16 REFERTA • PENHA DE ÁGUIA • CRUZ

Map pages 78-79

Distance: 6.5km/4mi; 3h

Grade: easy on the Levada Nova and the lower flanks of Penha de Águia; expert beyond. To reach the very top of 'Eagle Rock', you have to scramble; you must be sure-footed and have a head for heights. **Danger of vertigo on the descent from the summit!**

Equipment: walking boots (stout shoes will suffice if you are not climbing to the summit), sunhat, long trousers, picnic, water; extra cardigans and anorak in cool weather

How to get there: 🚌 53 or 78 from Funchal to Referta
To return: 🚌 53 or 78 from Cruz to Funchal

Short walk: Referta — Cruz. 4.7km/3mi; 1h. Easy. Stout shoes, sunhat, picnic, water. Access/return as above. Follow the main walk for 1h.

Alternative walk: See Alternative walk 15, page 81.

This walk explores the extraordinarily-named valley of Tem-te Não Caias ('Hold on — watch you don't fall!'), which we didn't find in the least bit vertiginous. Then we go on to climb Penha de Águia, which certainly is! From the pass at the top of 'Eagle Rock', all but the very long of leg and sure of foot will hang on for dear life trying to get down again...

Leave the bus at Referta, where there is a bar/shop, and walk a short way downhill to where the EN101 crosses the Levada Nova (opposite a road with a cul-de-sac sign). **Start walking** in the direction of Penha de Águia — the most prominent landmark in the north of the island. You may pass by a willow-worker's steaming vat almost immediately, before the levada takes you under the road via a tiny tunnel. Now you're in the valley of Tem-te Não Caias, noisy with the croaking of frogs. If a photo of the levada doesn't appeal to you (it usually has a sluggish flow and little water), then concentrate your camera on the tiny parcels of terracing below. Crops of every colour vie for space — bananas, peas, broad beans, runner beans, cabbages, onions, potatoes, sugar cane, wheat, barley. In the riverbed the ubiquitous willow flourishes.

In about **35min** you'll have reached a promontory with fine views of Penha de Águia ahead and the hamlet of Achada on a plain below (see photograph opposite). Take a break for a few minutes and work out your route up Eagle Rock. It climbs gently through the pines on the southern slopes, passes a solitary cow house, and then heads straight up to the easily-seen pass at the top. The massive rock doesn't look very impressive or forbidding from this angle, compared to other viewpoints on the island. But if you plan to climb it, perhaps that's just as well.

The aptly-named hamlet of Achada, from the Levada Nova in the Ribeira Tem-te Não Caias. 'Achada' means 'small plateau'.

Soon Macapez, Cruz and the rock off Porto da Cruz are seen ahead. In **50min** come upon a cobbled trail. Follow it downhill to the right (were you to cross straight over this trail, you would be on the faster-flowing Levada do Castelejo; Walk 15). The Levada Nova runs beside you on the left now. A cobbled trail comes in from the left (**56min**); ignore it and keep straight down. Porto da Cruz is just on your right now — an 'arm's length' away.

At **1h** you reach the EN101 at Cruz. Turn right downhill to the tiny electricity substation. (The Short walk ends here.) Some 20m/yds beyond the substation, cross the road and walk up a cobbled trail. After just a few metres/yards, bear right in front of a house, on a *very* narrow path. You've parted company with the Levada Nova, which continued beside the trail. Now there's a very narrow levada on your left. After bending into the valley, in a couple of minutes, a small banana grove pops up on your right. Your path up Penha de Águia begins *just at the end of this tiny grove,* on your left: look for a splodge of faded vermilion paint on a tree. Follow this path uphill, accompanied by the wonderful scent of pines (**P**16). Some eight minutes into the climb, the way is via steps hewn out of the rock: at the first fork go left; at the second fork go right and then go right again almost immediately. You pass just a few metres to the left of the lone *palheiro* that you spotted from the levada, earlier in the walk. In **2h10min** you reach the pass at the top, after a scramble up rock.

At the top you will be confronted by three paths: one goes straight ahead to a viewpoint over the sea, another goes right to a lookout over Porto da Cruz, and a third goes left to a triangulation point (589m on the map) and, we are told, down the west side of the rock. Luckily for Pat we did the climb in May and all three paths were impassable ... the most impenetrable jungle of lacerating ferns, gorse and blackberries we've ever encountered, well over our heads. Young Madeirans tell us they walk this route in summer ... and the first groups of walkers take machetes. So we'd suggest that you do this climb in late summer or autumn, when the rock-face may have been 'shaved' in your honour. As for us, we returned to the pass and shared our last apple. Pat wondering how/if she would get down. John wondering how/if he would get her down. We hadn't had any views from the top, except over the way we came (and that was vertiginous enough; presumably the others are like Cabo Girão, but without the protective railings). We were glad we'd done it but, for one of us, once was enough.

Return the same way to Cruz (**3h**), to pick up your bus.

Walk 17: The old levada path is well built and not at all vertiginous. All the steep drops are accomplished on steps, as you can see. While descending take a look at the intricate channels that have been cut to bring riverlets into the levada — someone either had a lot of time on his hands or a keen sense of humour!

Map begins on the reverse of the touring map and ends on page 44.

Distance: 7.5km/4.7mi; 2h45min   **See photograph opposite**

Grade: moderate descent of 900m/2350ft; sure-footedness required.

Equipment: stout shoes (walking boots preferable), sunhat, picnic, water; cardigans, long trousers and anorak in cool weather

How to get there: 🚐 taxi to the ice house (Poço da Neve) on the flanks of Pico do Arieiro

To return: town 🚌 11 to Funchal centre; see STOP PRESS, page 136.

Alternative walk: Pico do Arieiro — Short walk 18 — Poço da Neve — Funchal. Do Short walk 18 before this walk. Depending on whether you go to the first or second viewpoint, allow up to 10km/6.2mi; 4h. Grade, equipment, access/return as above.

What better than a walk combining the mountains *and* a levada? This excursion has it all — glorious views and a rushing watercourse to guide you. But wait till you've acquired your 'Madeira knees' — it's steep!

Start out at the domed ice house, 2km below Pico do Arieiro (*P*17). Scramble straight down the hill, to the lovely heath tree grove below. In the trees you meet a crossing track. Turn right on it and follow it up the Santa Luzia Valley towards Arieiro — the *opposite* direction from where you want to go! Across the valley you'll spot your onward route — a clear path climbing southwest up the ridge. Near the head of the valley, a track comes in from behind you, on your left (**30min**). Bear sharp left on it and cross the valley just above a dam. Then clamber up right onto the path you spotted earlier. Bear left and follow the path up to a pass (**40min**), where you bear right again, to join the very narrow Levada da Negra.

Turn left along this narrow blue ribbon and let the levada guide you to Funchal. A rocky moonscape, with knarled white heath tree limbs, alternates with ferny glens. Funchal reveals itself in the 'V' of the Ribeira de Santo António, and high peaks rise behind and beside you.

In just **2h** you pass through a gate and the descent from Arieiro ends, as you round a tributary of the river on a level path. Orange roofs glint through the canopy of the dense eucalyptus wood. In **2h05min** a levada shoots down to the left by a tiny waterhouse. Ignore it; keep straight on, along this narrow and slippery red-clay path. Beyond two further gates, in **2h30min**, you begin a new descent: turn left down a cobbled trail, with a levada on either side. Ten minutes later enjoy a superb view over Funchal— stretching from Boa Nova in the east to Cabo Girão in the west. Beyond a small hippy enclave, in only **2h45min**, you reach Barreira, the terminus for town bus 11.

18 PICO DO ARIEIRO • PICO RUIVO • ACHADA DO TEIXEIRA

Map on reverse of touring map; see also photograph pages 110-111.

Distance: 6km/3.7mi; 3h

Grade: expert. This is a very strenuous walk, with steep ascents and descents. You must be sure-footed and have a head for heights; **danger of vertigo!** 5 tunnels to pass (20min total). *Note that the walk is sometimes impassable due to landslides.*

Equipment: walking boots, raingear, anorak, cardigans, long trousers, whistle, sunhat, picnic, plastic bottle/water purifying tablets, torch

How to get there: 🚌 taxi to Pico do Arieiro. (It is usual to hire the taxi for the entire day. The driver would take you to Arieiro and wait there a couple of hours — in case landslides prevent you from completing the walk and you have to turn back. He would then drive on to Achada do Teixeira to collect you.) Alternatively, arrange for friends who are car touring to drop you off and collect you (Car tour 4).
To return: 🚌 the same taxi from Achada do Teixeira

Short walk: Pico do Arieiro — first or second viewpoint — Pico do Arieiro. 35min-1h15min. Stout shoes, sunhat. Easy, but some people will find even this path vertiginous. Remember, there is a stiff climb back up! Access/return: 🚌 car or taxi to Pico do Arieiro.

Alternative walk: Pico do Arieiro — Pico Ruivo — Queimadas — Santana. 16km/10mi; 6h. Grade, equipment, access as main walk. Do the main walk, then cross the car park at Achada. Go to the front of the building here and walk past it. Below you will spot the basaltic rock formation 'Homem em Pé'. Descend to pass it on the right, and continue down until you meet the road. Follow the road downhill to the viewpoint, from where the path continues (at the left side). *From here on the very steep path can be as slippery as ice. Even walking boots do not afford sufficient grip. Hang on to the heather trees to keep upright! Take this descent very slowly.* Some 1h20min from Achada, go through a gate and soon reach the upper house in the storybook setting of Queimadas Park. From the lower house (1h30min) take the steep cobbled road down to Santana (allow 1h30min). Turn right on the main road: 🚌 103 to Funchal leaves from the town hall (the building with a clock).

I f you're lashing out on a taxi to get to this walk, then try to make it a *very* early morning start and get to Pico do Arieiro at daybreak. The sun erupts like a ball of fire; shards of light cascade mauve and golden over mountaintops and valleys. The mists clear quickly but reluctantly, curling lovingly around the peaks, mere wisps and whispers and then they're gone. A shepherd appears suddenly from beneath a crest, shouldering a mighty load of firewood, sending goats and sheep scurrying between light and shade, as fluffy clouds throw shadows across the scrubby slopes.

Setting off from Pico do Arieiro at sunrise

The photograph on pages 110-111 gives you a good overview of your route. Here on Madeira's third highest peak (1818m/5965ft), you are far above the great Curral and Metade ravines. Most mornings the air is so clear that you can see to the heights above Porto Moniz. **Start the walk** by following the paved path from the viewpoint. It's easy walking at the outset, suitable for all visitors with stout shoes, but almost immediately you cross a very narrow spine between two ravines. This is a hint of the great chasms to follow on this trail linking the island's three highest mountains. Built in the late 1960s, Madeira's most famous mountain path is extremely well engineered, and the difficult stretches are protected by sturdy iron railings, opening up this glorious landscape to all visitors with the right clothing and lots of stamina. But, alas, all too often these railings are brought down by landslides, and there are **several dangerous passages** on the walk. Use your judgement, and **always be prepared to turn back**.

In **15min** you will reach the first viewpoint along the route (*P* 18). From here you can discern, to the northwest, a path running on the other side of the valley around the Torres, the second highest mountain on Madeira. The jagged teeth crowning this 'Peak of the Towers' hide Ruivo from view for most of the walk but, after you climb up left past the first outlook, you *can* see the island's highest peak — and, on a clear day, the outskirts of Funchal — from the second viewpoint, reached in **25min**. In **30min** a steep descent on stone steps begins; at the end of this descent, a rock archway will frame your photographs. Follow the path through the arch and soon look

right to get splendid views over the Metade Valley and the village of São Roque perched up on its *lombo*.

The first tunnel is met in **45min**; it passes through Pico do Gato ('Cat's Peak'). Past this tunnel, a goat gate on the right leads to a crumbled-away path round the Torres. Be sure to go left on the well-worn way to Ruivo. Almost at once you will see a basalt rock face **prone to landslides**. If the fences are not in place, this is the most dangerous part of the walk, often covered in fresh scree. ***Always be prepared to turn back!*** If you can continue, stop for a moment and look west for superb views of Pico Grande (Walk 4). Then go into the second tunnel at the end of the rock face (**1h**). The third and fourth tunnels follow on immediately. Just past the fourth, a grassy, broom-bedecked knoll commands spectacular views over Pico Grande and the expanse of the Paúl da Serra.

Enter the fifth and last tunnel in **1h15min**. At its exit, a path comes in from the right — the end of the derelict trail round Pico das Torres. (If you are doing the walk in reverse, be sure to go *sharp right* through a gate and into this tunnel about 30 minutes after leaving the Ruivo rest house. The main path *appears* to go straight ahead, complete with railings, but this is the path around the Torres. There is a signpost here pointing back to Ruivo, but *no* sign for Arieiro.) Continue left on the Ruivo path, which now skirts a cliff-edge with some caves. Soon the way is very like the trail between Ruivo and Encumeada: the broom gives way to gnarled heath trees which grace the sweeping vistas over the Metade.

It's a tiresome climb to the rest house below Ruivo (under **2h**), but you can buy a drink here before tackling the summit. From there, you will descend to the Achada do Teixeira in under 50 minutes (**3h**).

Walk 23: Not far along the path from Ruivo to Encumeada, you will be rewarded with this superb view out towards Pico Grande, setting for Walk 4.

19 QUEIMADAS • LEVADA DO CALDEIRÃO VERDE • SANTANA

Photographs pages 23, 32, 92

Distance: 18km/11.2mi; 5h15min

Grade: moderate, but only recommended for very experienced, very sure-footed walkers. The levada path is slippery and broken away in places. **Danger of vertigo throughout** (very severe drops on one side, adequately protected by sturdy railings, *but these often come down in storms*). Four tunnels (10min total). Steep descent to Santana.

Equipment: walking boots, torch, long trousers, 2 cardigans, anorak, whistle, picnic, plastic bottle with water purifying tablets

How to get there: 🚌 103 from Funchal to Santana and taxi from Santana to Queimadas (or by 🚗: see Short walk below).
To return: 🚌 103 from Santana to Funchal

Short walk: Queimadas — Levada do Caldeirão Verde — Queimadas. Follow the main walk as long as you like; return the same way. Or do Short walk 24-1 in reverse (see notes page 102). Take a picnic and cardigans, and wear *lace-up shoes with very good grip; sometimes the red clay soil here is like a skating rink!* Be sure to ask the taxi driver to return for you. 🚗: If you are travelling by car, see the notes for Car tour 4: you may prefer to park at Pico das Pedras (Short walk 24-1).

Think green. Think of rain forests ... of emeralds. This is Queimadas — a mossy paradise. And a bonus to this enchanting walk is a visit to Santana, one of Madeira's most picturesque villages. The houses are built in the 'old style', A-shaped and thatched right down to the ground, as a protection against the fierce northerlies.

Your bus stops for a ten-minute break at Poiso. A young fellow who had been on night duty at one of the hotels was travelling with us one morning. Eager to practice his English, he introduced us to the 'working man's breakfast' — a glass of sweet Madeira wine and a warm hard-boiled egg. It truly set us up for the drop in temperature once the bus descended past Ribeiro Frio to the north coast! This chill will be noticeable even on warm days, and this is *not* a suitable walk for winter months; perhaps as much as 2m/80in of rain falls at Queimadas in winter!

When you arrive at Queimadas Park (**P**19), you will find two charming *pousadas* (see page 36, 'Where to stay', and photograph page 32). **Begin the walk** by passing the lower houses, to discover yet another *pousada* — this one a miniature for the swans who live in the pools. Cross the wooden bridge and then turn right on the old Levada do Caldeirão Verde. The red clay underfoot is diabolically slippery — walk on the moss where you can. In **13min** pass through a gate, beyond which the path narrows. Four minutes later, be sure to leave the levada where it is broken away — the paths down and back up are slippery too.

The views are spectacular as you follow the levada westwards to one of the most remote parts of the island. After crossing two ravines — the Ribeira dos Cedros (**27min**) and the Ribeira da Fonte do Louro (**45min**) — you come in about **1h** to the first, very short tunnel. Two minutes beyond the exit, a path off right is signposted to 'Vale da Lapa', and Walk 20 leaves us here. Immediately you plunge into the second tunnel (five minutes). There is a path on the right at this tunnel exit, too, but we found it wasn't viable. The third tunnel lies just beyond this path; it's very low: *keep your head down* for the next two minutes. Not far past this third tunnel, you must leave the levada again to avoid an overhanging precipice.

Go through a final, very short tunnel in a couple of minutes and, 13 minutes later (**1h35min**), come to a spillway and a sluice. Climb up the path at the left of the

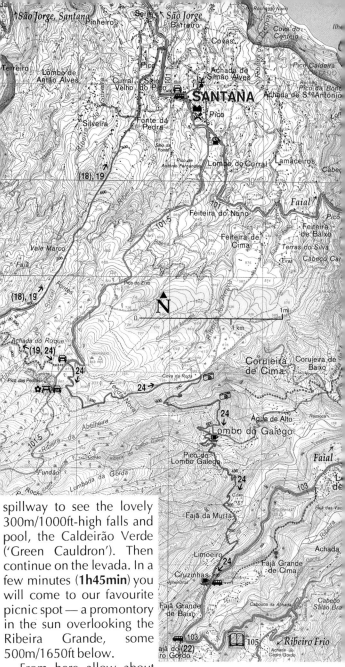

spillway to see the lovely 300m/1000ft-high falls and pool, the Caldeirão Verde ('Green Cauldron'). Then continue on the levada. In a few minutes (**1h45min**) you will come to our favourite picnic spot — a promontory in the sun overlooking the Ribeira Grande, some 500m/1650ft below.

From here allow about 3h30min to reach Santana. The road from Queimadas is shown by a green line on the map. Turn right on the EN101; the bus leaves from the town hall (the building with a clock; **5h15min**).

20 QUEIMADAS • VALE DA LAPA • ILHA DE SÃO JORGE

Map pages 90-91

Distance: 8.5km/5.3mi; 2h40min

Grade: moderate, with one fairly steep and slippery descent (20min)

Equipment: walking boots, long trousers, sunhat, extra cardigan, anorak, picnic, plastic bottle and water purifying tablets

How to get there: 🚌 103 from Funchal to Santana and taxi from Santana to Queimadas

To return: 🚌 103 from Ilha de São Jorge to Funchal

Alternative walk: Queimadas — Vale da Lapa — Queimadas. 10km/6.2mi; 2h45min. Quite easy. Access/return: 🚗 car or taxi to/from Queimadas Park (or Pico das Pedras; see Short walk 24-1, page 102).

Two walks in one: on this excursion you enjoy the shady meanderings of the Levada do Caldeirão Verde, and then you leave it for the sunny heights above São Jorge. From the tiny forestry station at Vale da Lapa, you have perhaps the island's finest view of the north coast villages from São Jorge round to Santana.

Begin by following Walk 19 for **1h**, when you pass through a very short tunnel (you won't need a torch). Two minutes beyond the tunnel exit, take the path off right (usually signposted 'Vale da Lapa'). The path curves sharp left at first and you come into a shady grove. Curve up to the right here (signposted 'Posto Florestal'). Some five minutes from the levada (**1h10min**) come to a fork: go straight ahead, not left. Ten minutes later you enjoy fine views over Ilha de São Jorge and Santana off to the right.

In **1h20min** you reach a small and lonely forestry house (the *posto florestal*). Enter its precincts via a gate; the resident hen and cockerel greet you, begging for biscuits. The gardens are charming, with tree ferns amongst the other plants. There is no track to this house, so the lone guard must come and go on

Walks 19, 20, 21: The Levada do Caldeirão Verde, with its typical heath-tree fences, is one of the most photogenic on the island. Do follow it for at least a short way.

Santana and the north coast, from the forestry house at Vale da Lapa

foot along the path we will now follow towards Ilha.

To leave the forestry house, pass to the left (west) of it on a fine cobbled trail, which soon reverts to path. Be sure to bend in a sharp U-turn to the right after a couple of minutes. In five minutes a path joins in from behind and to the right. It comes from a gate.* (Were you to go back, through the gate, you would have fine views over the Caldeirão Verde Levada and a lower levada in the same valley (Ribeira dos Cedros). The path was once a beautiful stone-edged levada, planted with hydrangeas. The channel has since been filled in with soil. The going gets extremely vertiginous after about ten minutes, however. Our timings do *not* include this possible detour.)

The descent is steep and slippery, often through a bower of heath trees and ferns. Some 25 minutes from the forestry house (**1h50min**) you arrive at a track. Turn right downhill on this *caminho de explotação* ('development track' — they are all over the island). The roadworkers tell us they are looking for *water*. Hard to believe. The track forks about 10 minutes downhill; go left, continuing the descent. Ten minutes later fork left downhill again, eventually coming onto asphalt. In **2h40min** you will arrive at Ilha church, from where the bus leaves.

*If you are climbing *from* Ilha to the forestry house (allow 2h for this ascent of 450m/1500ft), turn right on a narrow path just *before* this gate.

21 QUEIMADAS • CALDEIRÃO DO INFERNO • QUEIMADAS

Map pages 90-91 **Distance:** 15.5km/9.6mi; just over 5h

Grade: expert. Sure-footedness and a head for heights essential. **Danger of vertigo!**

Equipment: walking boots, long trousers, plastic rainhat, 2 cardigans, *waterproof* anorak or raingear, whistle, picnic, plastic bottle with water purifying tablets, torch

How to get there and return: 🚗 car or taxi to and from Queimadas Park (or Pico das Pedras; see Short walk 24-1, page 102). If travelling by bus, see Walk 19, page 89, and add 1h30min for the descent to Santana.

Alternative walk: Queimadas — Caldeirão Verde — Caldeirão do Inferno — Pico Ruivo tunnel — Fajã da Nogueira — EN103. 20km/12.4mi; 6h45min. Map continues on reverse of touring map. Grade, equipment, access as main walk. In addition to the hazards of the main walk, you must pass through a tunnel 2.4km/1.5mi long. *Each member of the party must carry a good torch.* Follow the main walk to the sun trap at the start of the Pico Ruivo Levada. Then return to the Pico Ruivo tunnel (15min). Plunge in. You exit about 40min later by booming waterfalls and clear pools, where the Ribeira Seca, coming down from its source on Pico das Torres, crashes into the levada. Another tunnel lurks beyond this one (12min). After these, the final few tunnels are a doddle. The levada is soon covered by workmen's jeep tracks. About 1h30min from entering the Ruivo tunnel you come to a track running down to the left. Descend it to the power station (1h; Walk 22 ascends this track). From the power station walk on to the EN103 (1h40min), to catch 🚐 103.

The awe-inspiring chasm of the Caldeirão do Inferno is hidden below the eastern flanks of Pico Canario and the northern escarpment of Ruivo — about as close to the heart of primaeval Madeira as you can get. As always, the levada builders have been there before you, taming the wilderness and opening your path.

Water for the Levada dos Tornos is captured at three main sources; the Caldeirão do Inferno is just one of them (see Walk 22, page 97).
Left: approaching the 'Inferno' ('Hell's Cauldron').
Right: at the source. Don't expect a roaring falls here; this is just surface water, pouring down from Pico Canario (1591m/5220ft). What **is** magnificent is the escarpment rising some 300m/985ft above you — at its most impressive after rain. Dwarfed by the rock walls lies a tiny levada channel — just a trickle in a grassy sun trap. It's so still you can hear the trees breathing.

The walk begins at Queimadas. Use the notes for Walk 19, page 89, to reach the Caldeirão Verde path at the spillway (**1h35min**). Have a look at the Caldeirão Verde waterfall, then leave the falls and turn left on the levada, crossing the spillway. Continue to a wonderful promontory in full sun, from where you overlook the valley of the Ribeira Grande (**1h45min**). Should you decide to have lunch here, you can have some fun with the aptly-named swifts! They'll spot you and, if you toss some small pieces of bread into the air, these acrobatic birds will catch them in mid-flight so quickly you'll hardly see them.

From here continue along the levada. Another impassable section of levada is encountered in under **2h**: slither down to the right and scramble back up again. In **2h05min** come to steps up to the left (the levada takes its source not far ahead). These steps are easily climbed, but coming down it's another story — a descent into nothingness, with no protective railings. You ascend 80m/260ft to a newer levada, the Levada do Pico Ruivo, at an altitude of 960m/3150ft (**2h13min**). Ahead of you is the Pico Ruivo tunnel (Alternative walk), 2.4km/1.5mi long. To the right of it is a large water tank. Walk along the edge of the tank (no problem, there are sturdy iron railings) and follow the levada towards the Caldeirão do Inferno. Just beyond the tank you have to walk under a waterfall and may get a dousing. Immediately afterwards, go through a short tunnel. You then pass through three more short tunnels and at **2h27min** come to roaring waterfalls in a cavern at the head

of the Ribeira Grande. This chasm is crossed via two very narrow bridges (see opposite), or you can descend to the riverbed below. Having described a U-turn in the valley, you pass through four more short tunnels and in **2h32min** you're at the setting shown here, the Caldeirão do Inferno, source of the Levada do Pico Ruivo. Relax at this magnificent picnic spot before returning to Queimadas (**5h**) ... or going on to Fajã da Nogueira.

Map on reverse of touring map   **Distance:** 14km/8.7mi; 5h45min

Grade: expert. Moderate climb/descent of 400m/1300ft on tracks.

Danger of vertigo during the second half of the walk, where the levada path is unprotected: sure-footedness and a head for heights essential.

Equipment: walking boots, long trousers, sunhat, cardigans, anorak, picnic, torch, whistle, plastic bottle with water purifying tablets

How to get there and return: 🚗 car or taxi to the power station at Fajã da Nogueira. (The walk is also accessible by 🚌 103 to the turn-off for the power station, but this adds a soul-destroying 4.5km each way.)

Shorter hikes: Fajã da Nogueira — Ribeira Seca or Pico da Nogueira — Fajã da Nogueira. Follow the main walk to 1h52min-point (3h40min return), or else climb the track that the main walk descends, to reach the viewpoint on Pico da Nogueira (2h20min return). Moderate hikes, each entailing a climb of 400m/1300ft (1h10min) on a track (no danger of vertigo; stout shoes would suffice). Access/return as main walk.

The Levada dos Tornos (Walk 7) was born here in the wilderness of Fajã da Nogueira in 1971, when the power station was inaugurated. Water for the Tornos is captured at three main sources. One source lies far to the northwest: an extremely long tunnel carries water from the Pôrco and São Jorge rivers directly to this power station. Another conduit is the rebuilt Levada da Serra do Faial e Juncal, which runs from the Juncal River to a pipe on Pico da Nogueira. The third source is the Caldeirão do Inferno (Walk 21): its waters flow through the Pico Ruivo tunnel to the same pipe. This walk explores the stretch between the tunnel and the pipe, whence both levadas plummet down to the power station.

Start the walk at the power station. Climb up the jeep track behind it. In **20min** you have superb views of the Torres ahead and Pico da Nogueira, with its pipe, on your left. In **35min** Pico do Arieiro is just ahead of you, with the Miradouro do Juncal also prominent. Five minutes later, a clearing with two enormous *paus brancos* (olive family) is passed on the left and, two minutes beyond this clearing, a track comes in from the left (your return route). You reach the Levada do Pico Ruivo (covered by a jeep track) in **1h10min**. Turn right (Alternative walk 21 follows this route in reverse). Beyond a couple of tiny tunnels, walking against the water's flow, you come to a first keepers' house (**1h12min**). Another follows on in three minutes. Both are especially well-placed picnic spots. In front of you a splendid cloak of emerald ridges coats the north side of the Ribeira Seca — the Cabeço da Fajã dos Vinháticos.

A first tunnel demanding use of your torch is met in **1h30min**, but it takes only three minutes to pass. In **1h40min** you come to a tunnel with railings for the levada workers; this takes 12 minutes. You'll hear the roar of the falls on the other side before you exit into the upper reaches of the Ribeira Seca, by crashing falls and clear pools — a superb picnic spot (**1h52min**).

From here return the same way to the track you climbed from the power station (**2h35min**), and now follow the

Opposite, top: This view towards the emerald ridges of the Cabeço da Fajã dos Vinháticos is alone worth the climb. Bottom left: The levada path is good (and will always be in good repair, since this is one of the island's most critical sources for water). However, the entire way is cut into the rock wall and is very narrow and sheer. As you may be able to see in the photograph, the wooden railings offer no more than psychological protection, and most of the cross-railings are missing. Bottom right: Throughout the walk your view plummets into gorges like the one shown here, the Ribeira da Fajã da Nogueira.

flow. From the outset, the path (see photograph page 96) is extremely vertiginous — far more so than the Caldeirão Verde path, and for longer stretches at a time. In and out of tributaries of the Ribeira da Fajã da Nogueira, in **3h05min** you are looking straight down it (photograph page 96). Still deep in the valley, by **3h35min** you find yourself on a mossy old levada, repaired and integrated into this new channel. In **3h55min** a tunnel on the right is drawing water from the bowels of Arieiro. Two minutes later, a filter clears the water running from this direction to the pipe. Now a track is ahead of you, with a tunnel to the right (**4h**). Not far into this high, wide tunnel, you cross the underground tank for both the Pico Ruivo and Juncal levadas, on a bridge. (It was not possible to build this large reservoir on the steep mountainside.) Listen to the rushing waters!

Just beyond the tunnel is the filtration tank for water running in from the Juncal, and this is where our levada explorations end (**4h07min**). Return through the tunnel and start down the track in front of it. (You might notice a path up on your right at the tunnel exit, and it goes where you are heading in half the time, but it is very narrow and broken away.) Less than ten minutes down the track, just before a keepers' house, reach a T-junction and turn up right on another track. This takes you back towards the top of Pico da Nogueira, to the outside of the underground tank (**4h35min**). There is a grassy verge here, another magnificent picnic spot, from where you overlook the Ribeira da Fajã da Nogueira and the Metade Valley. You're at 960m/3150ft; some 100m/330ft below, you can see the old levada that used to run between Balcões and Fajã da Nogueira, now completely crumbled away.

From this idyllic picnic spot, return down the track and, at the fork before the keepers' house, continue downhill. Pass the track off right to the keepers' house and another off to the right ten minutes later. In five minutes (**5h**) you ford the river, or cross it on the bridge made out of heather tree branches laid across pipes (similar to the one at the Caldeirão do Inferno shown on page 94). Now a ten-minute climb back uphill follows, until you meet your outgoing track, just above the mossy clearing with the enormous trees (during the entire walk you will have seen some of the oldest indigenous laurels and *paus brancos* on the island, some with trunks at least 8ft in diameter). Unfortunately, this stony dirt track is as irksome descending as it was on the ascent, and it will take another 35 minutes to return to the power station (**5h45min**).

23 ACHADA DO TEIXEIRA • PICO RUIVO • TORRINHAS PASS • ENCUMEADA

Map on reverse of touring map; photograph page 88; STOP PRESS page 136

Distance: 14km/8.8mi; under 6h

Grade: expert — a very strenuous walk, with steep ascents and descents. You must be sure-footed and have a head for heights: there are no protective railings at the (very few) exposed points; **danger of vertigo!** Expect to be caught up in mists. We have never encountered landslides en route, but don't discount the possibility — you might have to return to your departure point. *Important note:* Several paths radiate north and south from this walk, but only the route described is used regularly. Expert mountain walkers may wish to tackle some of the others (which we mention in passing), but we would not recommend any of them and so have not overprinted them in green on our map. Aside from being overgrown or broken away, some will be interrupted by roadworks.

Equipment: walking boots, raingear, anorak, cardigans, long trousers, whistle, compass, sunhat, picnic, plastic bottle with purifying tablets

How to get there: 🚌 103 from Funchal to Santana or 🚌 53, 78 or 103 from Funchal to Faial; taxi from Faial or Santana to Achada do Teixeira (pronounced 'Ah-**shah**-dah doh Tay-**shay**-rah)
To return: 🚌 6 from Encumeada to Funchal

Short walk: Achada do Teixeira — Pico Ruivo — Achada do Teixeira. 5.5km/3.4mi; 2h. Moderate climb and descent of 270m/885ft on a stone-paved path (with shelters and springs en route). Stout shoes, cardigan, anorak, sunhat, picnic, water. Access: as above (ask the taxi driver to wait for you or to return for you), or by 🚗 car (Car tour 4).

Blood red, then mauve; and finally silver and blue and gold. All was shadow; all was light. Nothing was real. Where sky ended and sea began, where mountains soared and clouds tiptoed down — all was merged into one. Sunrise at Pico Ruivo, the ultimate viewpoint on Madeira.

This is what you should aim for: take an afternoon bus to Santana or Faial and a taxi to Achada do Teixeira, then stay overnight at the Pico Ruivo rest house. Climb to the peak for sunrise; return to the rest house for breakfast, and *then* set out for Encumeada.*

Start out at the parking area at Achada do Teixeira (*P*23): turn west and take the paved path to Ruivo. About **40min** up, you enjoy wonderful views of Arieiro, the Torres and the path of Walk 18. You'll pass two springs and three shelters on the way, and then the path from Arieiro (Walk 18) comes in from the left. You reach the rest house in **45min** (drinks and snacks available).

*Or spend a night at the Pousada do Arieiro, perhaps visiting the ice house (Walk 17) and the Miradouro do Juncal in the morning. In the afternoon hike to Ruivo (Walk 18) for your overnight stay. (With existing bus connections, you can only do this walk as a day trip from Funchal if you walk *very* quickly, picnicking 'on the run'. Your best bet in this case is to alight from the early morning 103 bus at *Faial*, to save time.)

Five minutes above the house, you'll come to a saddle and a sign informing you that this path was built by the Tourism Department in 1949. At the left are steps to the Ruivo summit (1862m/6105ft), and the twin lookouts are reached in eight minutes. You'll want to linger up here for quite a while to see how many landmarks you can spot, including the Pico das Torres, Torrinhas Pass, Pico Grande, the Paúl da Serra, the Metade and Socorridos valleys, and the *pousadas* at Queimadas. To the northeast lies Porto Santo, floating like a cloud on the horizon.

From the summit, return to the signpost at the saddle. Turn down left here and strike out for Encumeada. Once in a while, you may see a vertical or horizontal daub of paint on a rock, but there is no other waymarking on this path, except just before and at Torrinhas Pass. Twenty minutes below the saddle, reach a gate and, almost at once, the valley leading down to Curral opens up before you, and you can see the higher hamlet of Fajã dos Cardos.

In **1h20min** walking the path forks; you will go left on stone steps, but first climb up slightly to the right, to see the fantastic views over the north coast, about 1300m/4250ft below. In **1h40min** come to a particularly good viewpoint over Curral's setting; now the path dips down south for a while, before resuming its westerly course. In **1h55min** start climbing to skirt a cone-shaped peak on your right … all the while enjoying the perfume of wild mint and thyme crushed underfoot.

At **2h05min** you'll reach a promontory with chasms to the left. Here, a disused path to Curral via Lombo Grande goes straight ahead; we go to the right. At **2h25min** climb down some steps and into another valley, from where you can again see again the north coast. You may also spot another derelict path, this one leading down right to São Jorge via Pico Canario, just before Pico das Eirinhas. Already you can see across the great valleys of the Ribeira Brava and São Vicente rivers, which split the island in two, and the new EN208 zigzagging up to the Paúl da Serra. The path squiggles endlessly, alternately giving views over the north and south of the island.

In **2h45min**, find a perfect promontory for lunch. Here two or three people can sit wedged in nature's rock-chairs and picnic while overlooking Curral das Freiras. This is just before you reach a fork in the path (marked by a large painted stone), where we turn right.* Pass through an

*The path on the left goes to Curral das Freiras and was described in the Third edition of this book. We have eliminated it from this edition

open gate and go down a few steps. Then the path turns left and descends steeply on worn stone steps beside a precipice, a **potentially dangerous** place, protected only by a meagre wire 'fence'. Stow away all unnecessary gear for this unpleasant descent! Then reach a grassy verge overlooking the north coast — an ideal picnic spot for groups of walkers.

At **3h** into the walk you will be confronted by the first of *many* flights of steep stone steps. These lead up to Torrinhas Pass. Soon signs point the way to Curral (back the way you've come, and then via the path described in the footnote) and Encumeada. You may also see a sign pointing to the threadbare remains of the old (1800s) trail to Boaventura via Fajã do Penedo; alas, it too, is derelict and scheduled to be replaced by the extension of the EN108 from Curral to Boaventura. The Encumeada path now takes you over Pico do Jorge — forever up and forever down — almost an hour, on giant-sized steps.

Beyond a signposted spring (at **4h30min**), a rock arch frames your photographs of the valleys of Serra de Água and São Vicente. Then descend through a glen of giant ferns beside a basalt escarpment at Pico do Ferreiro. At **4h55min** you may see an arrow pointing to a steep path down left: part of the 1800s trail between the Jardim da Serra and Encumeada, but no longer viable.

If you are lucky, this part of the walk, west of Pico do Jorge, can be glorious. But mists frequently descend by early afternoon, obscuring the valleys until you are well below 800m/2600ft. The mists will be welcome while you are climbing Pico do Jorge, and it is not difficult to follow the trail even in heavy mist and drizzle — just keep your wits about you and be that bit *more* vigilant.

Whatever the weather, you won't fail to be delighted by the 'orchard' of wild lily of the valley trees and the blue-and blackberry bushes bordering the hundreds of stone steps on which you descend to the end of the walk. By **5h50min** you reach a dirt track leading to the EN104 at Encumeada (1004m/3293ft). Walks 28 and 29 begin here, at the *miradouro* over the São Vicente Valley. Head south over the pass, to find the blue and yellow sign to Folhadal beside the Levada do Norte, starting point for Walks 26 and 27. Wait here for the bus if you're in good time; it is hardly ever late. Should you think you've missed it, telephone a Ribeira Brava taxi from the bar/restaurant.

---

because it was in *very poor* condition in the early 1990s and potentially dangerous in the Ribeira da Gomeira. It is also threatened by roadworks.

24 PICO DAS PEDRAS • COVA DA RODA • CRUZINHAS

Map page 91; photograph page 23; STOP PRESS page 136

Distance: 8.5km/5.3mi; 2h35min

Grade: moderate. The ascent at the end of the walk (180m/590ft) is tiring on a hot day.

Equipment: stout shoes (walking boots preferable), long trousers, anorak, sunhat, cardigans, picnic, water

How to get there: 🚌 53 or 78 from Funchal to Faial or 🚌 103 from Funchal to Faial or Santana; then taxi to Pico das Pedras
To return: 🚌 103 from Cruzinhas to Funchal

Short walks

1 Pico das Pedras — Queimadas — Pico das Pedras. 4km/2.5mi; 1h10min. Easy. Stout *lace-up* shoes with good grip (the path is level but can be *very* slippery), picnic, water. Access and return: 🚗 car or taxi (arrange return!) to Pico das Pedras. The levada lies 250m(yds) below the forestry house (Car tour 4); turn left here (if coming from the forestry house). Photograph page 23.

2 Pico das Pedras — Cova da Roda — Pico das Pedras. 3km/2mi; 1h30min. Moderate: the walk is level for a time, but there is a steep descent to Cova da Roda — and a corresponding climb back up! Stout *lace-up* shoes with good grip, picnic, water. Access and return: 🚗 car or taxi (arrange return!) to Pico das Pedras. Follow the main walk for 35 minutes and return the same way.

Alternative walk: Queimadas — Caldeirão Verde — Cruzinhas. 23km/14.3mi; 6h30min. Do Walk 19 first. On returning to Queimadas Park from the Caldeirão Verde, follow the levada to the crossing of the EN101-5 below the Pico das Pedras forestry house. Then do the walk described below. Grade, equipment, access: see Walk 19, page 89. To return: 🚌 103 from Cruzinhas to Funchal.

T ry to do this walk in September — on a day when it's not too hot for the ups and downs to be so tiring, but when the hydrangeas are still in bloom. You might even be lucky enough to see them in October, because they bloom later here than those around Monte. Quite simply, the hydrangeas bordering the levada between Pico das Pedras and the path to Cova da Roda are the most spectacular on the island! And the patchwork quilt of tiny terraces in these valleys is aglow with colour in early autumn.

Start the walk 250m/yds below the Pico das Pedras forestry house, where the EN101-5 crosses the Levada do Caldeirão Verde. Turn right (when coming down from the forestry house; a left turn leads to Queimadas); there is a sign here for 'Faial'. Stroll beside the levada under the shade of holm oak, eucalyptus and a 'forest' of gloriously-blue hydrangeas. After **10min** turn left down a track, with the levada gurgling beside you on your left. Five minutes later, turn down left again; don't follow the narrow levada straight ahead — the path is too overgrown. In **20min** a track comes in from behind you and to the right: ignore it and continue downhill. Another track off to the right, five minutes later, should also be ignored. In **30min** you reach a lone house on the left. Continue downhill (breaks in the trees afford some superb views to the right, towards Penha de Águia) for another 400m/yds, to a crossroads (**35min**). This is Cova da Roda. A track goes left to Santana and the one we have been descending continues ahead to Faial. The walk turns down right here. As you descend, look out left for an old stone-laid trail on the opposite side of the valley, and for the path leading down to it. (If you miss this path, your track will end at a small tunnel bored for water exploration; just retrace your steps for about 200m/yds to find the path, on your *right*.) You descend to a first stone bridge (**45min**). Ten minutes later you get the best views of 'Eagle Rock', before descending into the next valley.

Pass through Lombo do Galego, and ignore a road off to the left: instead, bear sharp right by a derelict house (with its roof at 'street level'), keeping to the old trail. A second stone bridge is met a couple of hundred metres/yards downhill, just beyond a waterfall (**1h30min**). As you continue towards the next valley, stop to admire the harmony of your surroundings: the terracing and multi-coloured houses to your left, the mass of Eagle Rock in front of you, with the red roofs of houses clustered around its base, and the blue of the sea cupped on either side of it.

Another glen introduces the third bridge (**1h55min**), and a further descent takes you to the fourth bridge at Fajã da Murta. Five minutes later you are at the fifth bridge (**2h05min**), which crosses the Ribeira Seca — one of the three great streams flowing to Faial. From here it's a 30-minute climb to Cruzinhas and the EN103 (**2h35min**). The bus stops just to the left (no *'paragem'* sign).

The Ginjas waterhouse (Walk 28) is one of many delightful cottages where the levada workers keep their tools. Many have lovingly-tended gardens, full of flowers and bordered by neatly-manicured hedges.

25 LEVADA DO FURADO: RIBEIRO FRIO • LAMACEIROS • PORTELA

Distance: 11km/6.8mi; 3h30min   **Other photos pages 19, 80-81**

Grade: moderate, but only for the agile! **Danger of vertigo** (but the worst drops are usually well protected by iron railings).

Equipment: walking boots or stout shoes that grip on slippery surfaces, long trousers, anorak, sunhat, cardigans, plastic bottle and water purifying tablets, picnic, whistle

How to get there: 🚐 103 from Funchal to Ribeiro Frio
To return: 🚐 20, 53 or 78 from Portela to Funchal

Short walks

1   Ribeiro Frio — first steep drops on the levada — Ribeiro Frio. 30min. Stout shoes, cardigan. Access and return: 🚐 103 from Funchal or 🚗 to Ribeiro Frio. Follow the main walk for 15 minutes, then return.

2   Ribeiro Frio — Balcões — Ribeiro Frio. 2km/1.3mi; 40min. Easy. Stout shoes, cardigan. Access and return: 🚐 103 from Funchal or 🚗 to Ribeiro Frio. See Car tour 4, page 29, and photograph page 19.

Alternative walks

1   Ribeiro Frio — Balcões — Portela. 13km/8mi; 4h10min. See Car tour 4, page 29, to walk to Balcões, then do the main walk below.

2   Ribeiro Frio — Lamaceiros — Levada da Serra. You can join the Levada da Serra at the Lamaceiros waterhouse and continue for as long as you like: from Lamaceiros, follow the levada to the Santo da Serra waterhouse (30min). Then refer to Walk 10, page 69.

3   Ribeiro Frio — Portela — Funduras — Ribeira de Machico. 19.5km/ 12mi; 6h. Grade, equipment, access as above. Follow the main walk to Portela. From the front of the Restaurante Casa da Portela, follow the Levada da Portela eastwards, along the unmade road running parallel to it. Now refer to the map on pages 78-79. After 15min, ignore the track up right to the radio mast. At the end of the levada you come to a fine coastal outlook. Here turn right uphill. After a climb of five minutes, the track gradually descends. In 1h come to a strong bend to the right, where a sign on the left indicates 'Funduras/ Ribeira de Machico'. Five minutes later, at a crossroads (called 'Funduras'), bear right downhill (signposted 'Ribeira de Machico'), with the valley of the Ribeira das Cales on your left. In 1h45min ignore the track going back to the left (signposted 'Ribeira das Cales/Maroços'). In just over 2h the road becomes metalled, and you meet the first houses of Ribeira de Machico. Continue to the main road (EN101; 2h30min). Return on 🚐 20, 53 or 78.

T his is a walk to which we return again and again. The views are spectacular, and the steep drops add a touch of excitement. It's not dangerous if you have proper walking equipment and go carefully. But anyone can come along with us for just a short way, to marvel at the play of light and shade over rocks and fountains, laurel and heath trees — this is what characterises the first part of the walk. The second part of the walk, beyond the Lamaceiros waterhouse, is completely different. You cross sunny pastures, enjoying panoramas of majestic mountains, proud valleys, and the tranquillity of the north coast villages in the distance.

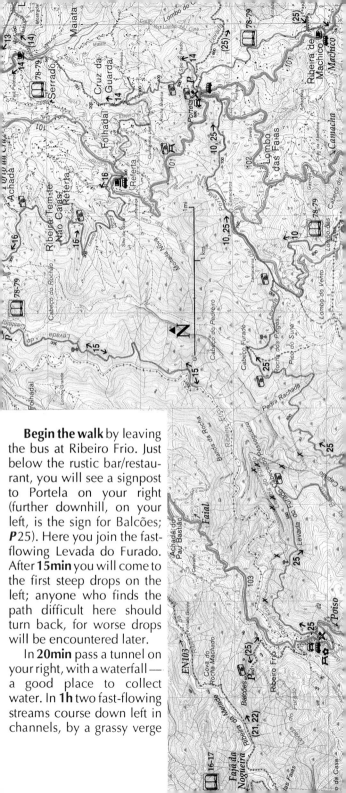

Begin the walk by leaving the bus at Ribeiro Frio. Just below the rustic bar/restaurant, you will see a signpost to Portela on your right (further downhill, on your left, is the sign for Balcões; *P* 25). Here you join the fast-flowing Levada do Furado. After **15min** you will come to the first steep drops on the left; anyone who finds the path difficult here should turn back, for worse drops will be encountered later.

In **20min** pass a tunnel on your right, with a waterfall — a good place to collect water. In **1h** two fast-flowing streams course down left in channels, by a grassy verge

— a splendid picnic spot. A few minutes later, photographers will be in their element: stepping stones bridge the levada, and the play of light and shade is intensified. After passing through a small cleft in the rock, watch for a red arrow alerting you to the first of six deviations from the levada: it is easier to cross the riverbed than to follow the channel. Soon there are splendid views of the high peaks, especially the jagged crown of the Torres.

At about **2h15min** you will pass through a very short tunnel. Just before it, a path on the left doubles back over the levada and climbs Pico da Suna (45min up and back down). One minute beyond this tunnel you come to a precipice, where the *very narrow* levada path is cut into the Suna escarpment. This lasts for ten minutes.

By **2h40min** you'll reach the Lamaceiros waterhouse and look out east to São Lourenço. (From here you can go on to the Levada da Serra; Alternative walk 2). About 30m/yds past the waterhouse, turn left down a path to find the narrow Levada da Portela. Follow it to a forestry house, and here join a track at the right (shown on the map as a finished road; see footnote page 70). Descend gently, with marvellous views of Faial, Penha de Águia and Porto da Cruz, settings for Walks 13-16. When the levada disappears, stay on the road. After 130m/yds, go left on a

grassy path to find the levada on your left and fenced-in pastures on your right. At a fork, bear right, following the levada (now on your right). You'll come to a derelict waterhouse. Go left here: slippery earthen steps edged with lilies and hydrangeas take you down to the EN102. Portela's restaurant (**3h30min**) is downhill to the left; the bus stops just south of it, but on the *EN101* (signposted to 'Machico'). Or continue to Ribeira de Machico (Alternative walk 3).

Light and shade on the fast-flowing Levada do Furado

Map on reverse of touring map

Distance: 14km/8.7mi; 4h

Grade: Expert. Sure-footedness and a head for heights essential. **Danger of vertigo!** Very narrow levada paths, many of them unprotected, and at least two potentially hazardous scree areas; one *very* long tunnel.

Equipment: walking boots, long trousers, good torch *for each member of the party*, whistle, sunhat, plastic bottle with water purifying tablets, picnic, 2 cardigans, anorak, rainhat

How to get there: 🚌 6, 139 or 150 from Funchal to Encumeada. Or by 🚗: park at the bar/restaurant or the viewpoint at the pass.
To return: 🚌 6 from Encumeada to Funchal, or 🚗 hire car

Short walks

1 Encumeada — waterfall (40min) — Encumeada. 6km/3.7mi; 1h 20min. Easy, but **danger of vertigo**; sure-footedness and a head for heights essential. Stout shoes, sunhat. Access/return as main walk.

2 Encumeada — Folhadal — Encumeada. 7km/4.3mi; 2h. Moderate. Equipment, access/return as main walk. *Take a torch* (two tunnels: 10min and 15min). Follow the main walk to the 14min-point, where you go right into a tunnel, to continue on the Levada do Norte. (We'll never forget our first walk here: we approached the tunnel — it was doorless then — to find what looked like a washing machine gone mad. Thick white 'foam' was pouring out of it — fog, rushing through from the other side. If you arrive to find this fog, it doesn't bode well for this short walk; you probably won't see a thing. Do Short walk 1 instead.) The second long tunnel looms ahead after 40min. It looks very low, but you will find, once inside it, that you can stand erect. At the exit (55min walking) you are at Folhadal, with splendid views of Ruivo and the valley leading to São Vicente, as well as the Folhadal waterfalls on your left.

Power and majesty. These may be your first impressions when you step onto the levada at Encumeada Pass. You are at the centre of the deep north/south cleft that splits the island. The great peaks rise in the east; the magnificent valley of Serra de Água lies to the south. And at your feet, the Levada do Norte, 1.5m/5ft deep and just as wide, surges along its course in a massive concrete channel. You're bound for Cascalho — a primaeval wonderland, known only to goats, levada builders and a very, very few guides and walkers. It's a hidden bowl of waterfalls where the Ribeira da Ponta do Sol gathers its strength; the torrent now feeds the Levada das Rabaças (1970), a 'tributary' of the Levada do Norte.

When the bus reaches Encumeada, the levada is just a few steps up from the road, opposite the bar/restaurant, on the south side of the pass. **Start the walk** by following it westwards, past the well-kept keepers' house. You'll be amazed by the abundance of vegetation: conifers of every description, heath and hawthorn, with a tangle of laurel,

Approaching the keepers' house on the Levada das Rabaças, with the Paúl da Serra rising behind it

azaleas, lilies, hydrangeas, and myriad wild flowers. If you're lucky enough to come in June, you'll see the splendid cornflower-blue 'Pride of Madeira' in all its glory. In **12min** you come to the promontory of Lapa do Galho (**P**26): from here you enjoy fine views down over the valley and the south coast. You can also see the levada continuing to the east and emptying into the metal pipe down to the power station (inaugurated in 1953). There are 50km/31mi of channels north of here (including 11km/6.8mi of tunnels). From the power station the water flows on in another 35km/22mi of channels (7km/4.5mi of tunnels) to irrigate the terraces of Ribeira Brava and Câmara de Lobos* (see Walk 6).

Past the promontory the levada forks (**14min**; here a levada workers' road comes up from behind you, on the left). Keep left, now following the Levada das Rabaças — or open the door to the tunnel on your right, if you are doing Short walk 2 and staying on the Levada do Norte. In **23min** you pass the overgrown path down left to Pico Redondo (Walk 27). Five minutes later, beyond a gate, you cross one of the many screes on the walk (caused by the roadworks on the EN204, but all are shored up and perfectly safe). You will have noticed by now that the vegetation is more sparse: roadworks, levada works, and fires, all in the late 80s and early 90s, have almost totally destroyed what was once perhaps Madeira's most beautiful levada. And, of course, with the vegetation gone, the entire route is far more vertiginous than it once was. The ferns and broom are bounding back, and the *levadeiros* are planting many flowers, but the loss of the myriad old trees is heartbreaking.

In **40min** a waterfall on the right heralds a short tunnel

*See photograph and caption on page 57.

(3min to pass). Seven minutes later, you reach the lonely keepers' house, above the Pousada dos Vinháticos (see opposite). In **55min** come to *the* tunnel — not for the claustrophobic! The path is good, the tunnel wide and tall, but it takes *at least 30 minutes to get through it.*

You exit from the tunnel at a large basin and then cross a spillway to join the levada path. Soon reach the first scree. Levada works ensured that the path was in good condition in the 1990s but, *if you find the scree is not shored up, the walk must be abandoned now.* The name 'Cascalho', by the way, conjures up visions of cascading waterfalls: but the name really means gravel or *scree!* Count yourself lucky if you reach the bowl of Cascalho (**1h50min**) before the mists fall... In our experience the 'curtain comes down' on this dramatic setting at the stroke of noon. Take any photographs *immediately,* before you stop for lunch. One of the best picnic spots is the western side of the bowl, just before the levada narrows and disappears round a bend.

If your return walk is misty, the sheer drops to the right will be hidden from view; you will have time to notice another indigenous Madeiran tree — the white-barked *pau branco* (olive family). Its gnarled and grotesque arms provide your only contact with 'reality', as you return to Encumeada (**4h**) almost literally suspended in clouds...

On a stormy day, a sun-shaft alights on Pico Redondo (Walks 26, 27; near Picnic 26)

27 ENCUMEADA • PICO REDONDO • POUSADA DOS VINHÁTICOS

Map on reverse of touring map; see photographs page 109 and cover; see also STOP PRESS page 136.

Distance: 4km/2.5mi; 1h45min

Grade: very strenuous; sure-footedness is essential.

Equipment: walking boots, sunhat, long trousers, whistle, cardigan, anorak, picnic, water

How to get there: 🚌 6, 139 or 150 from Funchal to Encumeada. (If you are staying at Vinháticos, we suggest that you take a bus from there to Encumeada and do the walk as described, rather than climb up to Pico Redondo from Vinháticos. From the *pousada* the route is difficult to find whereas, descending, all the other paths join in from behind you.)
To return: 🚌 6 from the Pousada dos Vinháticos to Funchal

The grass on Pico Redondo is just as soft and green — or, in summer and autumn, as golden — as it looks every time you walk west on the Levada das Rabaças and pass this inviting knoll, shown in the photograph on page 109. If you've the agility to get there, it's a delightful place to sit and watch the clouds roll by.

Start out as in Walk 26 (page 107), passing the tunnel entrance in **14min**. Keep left on the levada and, in **23min**, find the path out left to Pico Redondo, half hidden in broom trees. *Hang on to the trees while making this very steep descent!* The path, which is often masked by fallen trees and ferns, goes straight out to the peak. You'll come to a fence in about **50min**. Go through the gate, remembering to close it behind you. You'll be up with the sheep, at the top of the knoll, in under **1h**.

When it's time to leave, return to the fence and follow it back the way you came. Soon you'll see a gap (or a new gate) off to the left (southwest, downhill). Make for it, on a faint path. Beyond the gap/gate, the path heads downhill, but soon goes left. Come to a T-fork in about 15 minutes and go right to a cow house, where you take a sharp left. Zigzag through freshly-cultivated plots to reach and cross a very narrow levada. The path drops down on 'steps' beside this levada; once at the foot of the steps, find it again, heading left. Ten minutes past the levada crossing, fork right alongside a pipe, to cross another narrow levada in two minutes. Follow the narrow path at the right of this levada all the way to the EN104 at the north side of the *pousada* (50min from the gap/gate at Pico Redondo; **1h45min**). What better spot to end a walk?

28 ENCUMEADA • PINÁCULO • CARAMUJO • ENCUMEADA

Map on reverse of touring map

Distance: 18.5km/11.5mi; 6h

Grade: for experienced walkers. A strenuous ascent of 500m/1640ft; sure-footedness essential. **Danger of vertigo** on the levada to Encumeada and four long tunnels (35min in all). **NB**: *Bus times are very tight!*

Equipment: walking boots, long trousers, sunhat, cardigans, anorak, picnic, plastic bottle with water purifying tablets, whistle, torch

How to get there and return: 🚌6 from Funchal to Encumeada and back, or 🚗: park at the viewpoint on the north side of the pass.

Alternative walk: Lombo do Mouro — Pináculo — (Caramujo) — Bica da Cana. If friends are willing to play taxi, you can avoid the worst of the climb *and* the tunnels. See Car tour 5: a diversion could be made from Encumeada up the EN204 to the 'Bica da Cana' signpost (3.3km), where the path leaves the road. You would pick up the notes at the 1h15min-point. You could then re-meet your transport on the Paúl da Serra, at the Bica da Cana house (**P**28): see text on page 112, and follow the path for 10min up left to Bica da Cana (if you like, first go on to Caramujo and then return to this path). Arrange to meet by entrance of the old trail to the house (see Picnic 28). Allow 5km/3mi; 1h45min (9km/5.6mi; 3h05min to include Caramujo). Moderate; sure-footedness essential.

A nother of our very favourite walks on the island, absolutely gorgeous in its own right … *and* affording a splendid panorama of the great peaks — settings for Walks 4, 5, and 18. You're just on the eastern flanks of the Paúl da Serra, and you'll enjoy the laughter of a cascading levada and the falls that feed it. Myriad bright flowers line the route, and equally bright butterflies dart amongst them.

Giant heath trees on the Levada da Serra below Bica da Cana frame the view east to the great peaks, setting for Walks 4, 5 and 18. Pico Grande can be seen at the right, peeking between the branches. Behind it, to the left, stands Arieiro. Gato is the lone pointed peak further to the left, followed by the jagged Torres and, finally, Ruivo.

But the price to be paid is a 1h15min slog along the EN204 and then a stiff climb up to the 'Pinnacle'.

Begin the walk on the north side of the pass at Encumeada; follow the EN204. You climb above the Norte and Rabaças levadas (Walk 26), with a bird's-eye view of their sinuous meanderings. All around you, the mountains are clothed in the giant heath trees that give them their characteristic 'velvety' appearance. In under **1h15min** you reach a signpost on the right, 'Encumeada/Bica da Cana'. Climb steps here up to the Levada do Lombo do Mouro and follow it to the right, until you come to a steep path on your left. It takes you up … and up to the Levada da Serra (**1h50min**).

Relax now — and enjoy some good and easy walking along a grassy path, with magnificent views over the north coast and the valley leading to São Vicente. You'll soon see Pináculo rising up ahead to the right and meet the giant basalt pinnacle in **2h15min**. Just past Pináculo is our favourite lunch spot: here you can sit in long golden grasses ablaze with foxgloves and butterflies, beneath waterfalls foaming down a high and mossy basalt rock face. The soft valley of the Ribeira Seca lies before you, leading down to São Vicente and the chapel of Nossa Senhora de Fátima. Hawks circle watchfully above.

Continuing beside the levada, in **2h25min** come to a signposted path up left to Bica da Cana; ignore it and continue ahead (signposted to Caramujo). In **2h30min** the levada's source is met: forge ahead along the path — shoulder deep in lime-green vegetation. (*Keep an eye open, if you are being met at Bica*, for a blue-painted '+' on a rock on the ground. From here follow a good, but overgrown path on your left almost straight up to Bica; you will spot its triangular 'no hunting' sign on the plateau.)

The continuing path to Caramujo alternates between stone trail, riverbed, and grass. You have to push your way through giant heath tree bowers and broom. Look out for the old Caramujo houses, or you'll miss them. They are on the right, by a cultivated field. In **3h30min** the path disgorges onto the EN208, 300m/yds past an overgrown path off right to Caramujo. Head right, downhill, and meet the Ginjas waterhouse (drawing on page 103) in **4h30min**. Turn right on the levada here and follow it to Encumeada (**6h**). For part of the way you are doing Alternative Walk 26-2 in reverse. When you're not in the gloom of a tunnel or suffering an attack of vertigo, the levada's ferny glens, agapanthus, and fine views to the peaks are a joy.

29 ENCUMEADA • LEVADA DO LOMBO DO MOURO • RIBEIRA BRAVA

Map begins on the reverse of the touring map and ends below; photograph page 32; STOP PRESS page 136.

Distance: 15.5km/9.6mi; 5h40min

Grade: expert at present (but see STOP PRESS). Sure-footedness and a head for heights essential. Very strenuous, with a climb of 300m/985ft to start (but see 'How to get there' below), a *very* difficult descent to the levada (currently), and a steep descent of 1300m/4265ft to Ribeira Brava. **Danger of vertigo!**

Equipment: walking boots, long trousers, whistle, sunhat, cardigans, anorak, picnic, plastic bottle with water purifying tablets

How to get there: 🚐6 from Funchal to Encumeada, or 🚗: private transport to the path above the Lombo do Mouro house (4.3km from Encumeada on the EN204; see STOP PRESS).

To return: 🚐6, 7, 80, 107, 139, 150 from Ribeira Brava to Funchal

The Lombo do Mouro, a dinosaur's back of a ridge, is the setting for a delightful levada walk ... but save it until you've acquired your 'Madeira knees' — the descent to Ribeira Brava will leave them quaking!

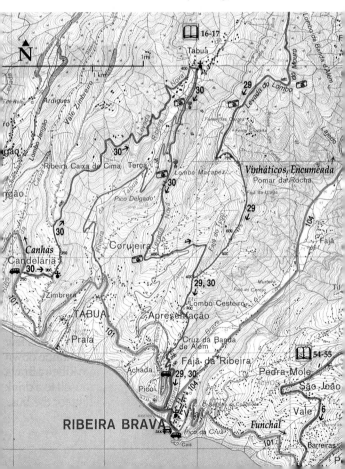

To **start out**, follow Walk 28 to the signpost 'Bica da Cana' (**1h15min**). Stay on the road and, 20 minutes later, you'll come to a promontory on the left. Walk to the edge: you look straight down on the Lombo do Mouro house, surrounded by a lovingly-built, almost circular stone wall. Once this was an idyllic single-storey stone cottage for hunters and wayfarers. Descend to the house (see STOP PRESS on page 136); you're there in **1h55min** or less.

Now bear right on the levada. You cross two screes caused by roadworks in the 1980s; they are perfectly safe now, but vertiginous nonetheless. There are fine views towards Pico Grande (Walk 4), Achada da Pinta (Walk 5) and the Arieiro/Ruivo trail (Walk 18). Go through a goat gate in **2h25min** and then perhaps take a break in the tall golden grass — a delightful spot to picnic, with orange butterflies pursuing the purple thistles and foxgloves, and the levada surging down beside you.

In **2h55min** you come into the eucalyptus zone, so you know that you have already dropped to below 900m/ 2950ft. Five minutes later the levada describes a wide curve to the left and descends very steeply. Watch your footing, and try to ignore the goats glaring down at you from the embankment up on your right. Soon, if you climb this bank, you can look down on Tabua's levada (Walk 30). Over to the left are the pines of Boa Morte (Walk 6).

In **3h30min** leave the levada to join an unmade track on the left (the way ahead is blocked by a rock); you can rejoin the levada in a minute. But the track persists beside you and, in **4h10min**, you're forced to join it. Follow it until it turns off right at a junction of levadas. Here walk straight ahead, down earthen steps, towards houses and another track. The levada is still beside you. Go left on this new track (**4h15min**), with the levada on your left. Soon rounded stones reveal themselves beneath the soil, and you realise that you are on a centuries-old trail. In a Madeiran version of the labours of Hercules, women are on their hands and knees *weeding* between the galaxy of stones. Ignore any turnings off this steep trail (but notice, at **4h30min**, a track crossing by an electricity transformer inscribed with '1990-02-26' on its concrete base: about 60m/yds below this crossing track, Walk 30 comes in from the right, just in front of a garage. You have to walk a few paces to the right to see the levada here). Continue down to the EN101 (**5h20min**). Turn left down into Ribeira Brava (**5h40min**) and collapse into a café; treat youself to a drink and your knees to a massage, while waiting for the bus.

Map page 113
Distance: 10km/6.2mi; under 3h10min
Grade: moderate, but a very steep descent. **Danger of vertigo!**
Equipment: stout shoes or walking boots, long trousers, sunhat, picnic, water; extra cardigan and anorak in cool weather
How to get there: 🚌 80 or 107 from Funchal to Candelária
To return: 🚌 6, 7, 80, 107, 139, 150 from Ribeira Brava to Funchal

White iris, broom and sugar cane in springtime; hayricks, sweet chestnuts and blackberries in autumn. Take your pick of seasons to enjoy the fertile valley of the Ribeira da Tabua.

Ask the bus conductor for Candelária, the *third* stop after you round the point past the junction to coastal Tabua. The second stop is at the Quinta Heidy; you get off at the *next* one. A few paces north of the stop, find stone steps leading up and *south* — by telephone wires. To **start the walk**, climb up here, joining a road in **3min** (it began at the bus stop by the Quinta Heidy). Follow the road uphill until you come to an old stone-laid trail at a crossroads (**12min**), where 'Levada Nova' is written on a wall. Turn left (north) up the trail (a chapel, hidden behind a house, is on your right) and climb steeply for about another 20 minutes, until the trail crosses the levada (**32min**). At your left will be a house with a vine trellis on the roof.

Turn right on the levada and soon you will be heading north. Beyond a sugar cane grove, you'll have to ford two very wet spillways where the river crosses the levada; at the second, you are at inland Tabua (**1h20min**). From here head southeast in the valley. Almost at once steps take you up to a road. Cross it and descend to the levada on the other side. The best views of the valley are to come.

Poplars grace the valley of the Ribeira da Tabua.

After passing through a cut in the basalt cliffs (**1h30min**) where stepping stones bridge the levada, you find the best lunch spot: a grassy verge shaded by fig trees, overlooking the river valley, its pools, poplars and hay-ricks. But along here the path is extremely exposed, and those prone to vertigo may have to wade in the channel!

A short tunnel (**1h37min**; no torch needed) takes you into a side valley. Soon pass a grassy knoll (**1h40min**) on the right, with a superb outlook over coastal Tabua, another fine picnic spot. In under **2h** the levada disappears beneath a walkway. Turn left up concrete steps, to a house in Corujeira, where a road descends to the EN101. Walk down the road a few paces and continue the walk on the (narrower) levada on the other side. You'll round the Ribeira da Caldeira and then meet a stone-laid trail (**2h15min**; Walk 29). Turn right and continue *very* steeply downhill to the EN101 and Ribeira Brava (**3h10min**).

31 RAMBLES AROUND RAPOSEIRA

See photographs pages 17, 29 and 30; see also map on page 121 and touring map.

Grade: very easy   **Distance:** see individual walk suggestions.

Equipment: stout shoes, sunhat, picnic, water

How to get there: 🚌 107 from Funchal to Raposeira, or 🚗 hire car
To return: 🚌 80, 107, 139, 150 to Funchal, or back to your car

The infrequently-visited southwest of the island will soon be opened up to walkers by new hotels (see page 36). Meanwhile, if you don't mind a long drive or bus ride, here are some suggestions for rambles. Throughout, you will be on the sun-drenched plains just above the coast and will delight in the clouds dancing patterns over the bracken-gold flanks of the Paúl da Serra.

Short walk: Raposeira — Paúl do Mar overlook (**P31**). See Picnic 31, page 15, and photograph page 17.

Alternative walks: Both follow the Levada Calheta—Ponta do Pargo (called 'Levada Nova' on the map). You stroll under pine and eucalyptus, by ferny glens and banks of lilies. While there is ample shade, much of the route is exposed, so adequate sun protection is required. Those travelling by bus should alight at Raposiera church. 🚗: There are several places to park by the quiet EN101, for example just west of Raposeira church, at the crossroads down to Fajã da Ovelha and Paúl do Mar.

1 Raposeira — east on the levada. Start out on the levada just below (south of) Raposeira church, and turn left. You can leave the levada for the EN101 at Prazeres (4.7km/3mi; 1h), Lombo dos Moinhos (9km/5.6mi; 2h), or the power station above Calheta (20.5km/12.7mi; 4h). Beyond the power station you join Walk 32, from where you continue to Loreto (26.5km/16.5mi; 5h30min; notes and map pages 120-121). See photograph page 29.

2 Raposeira — west on the levada. Start out on the levada just below (south of) Raposeira church, and turn right. You can go as far as Ponta do Pargo (10.5km/6.5mi; 2h15min) or, as seen on the touring map, leave at any of the places where the levada crosses or approaches the EN101 (eg, São João, shown in the photograph on page 30).

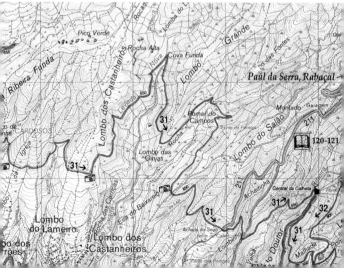

32 CAMPO GRANDE • LEVADA DO PAÚL •
RABAÇAL • LORETO

Distance: 15km/9.3mi; 4h45min

Grade: moderate, with a **possibility of vertigo** on the levada

Equipment: stout shoes (walking boots are preferable), sunhat, anorak, cardigans, picnic, plastic bottle with water purifying tablets, torch

How to get there: 🚌 107 from Funchal to the Canhas taxi rank, 1.5km west of Canhas, at the 'Recta das Canhas' bus stop ('**Ray**-tah dahs **Kahn**-yahs'). As soon as you reach Canhas, look on your right for a statue representing the *first* station of the cross (by the church), and start counting: just past the *fourteenth* station, there is a large monument to St Theresa. Leave the bus here; the taxi rank is opposite. Ask the driver to take you to 'Cristo Rei, Campo Grande' (**Kreesh**-toh **Ray**, **Kam**-poh **Grahnd**).
To return: 🚌 80, 107, 139 or 150 from Loreto to Funchal

Short walks

1 Levada do Paúl. Walk as far as you like from Cristo Rei along this levada; perhaps to the caves and back. 5km/3mi; 1h30min. Grade and equipment as above (but no torch needed). Best access is by 🚗 (a detour on Car tours 5 and 6). *Note that the path may be very wet!*

2 Rabaçal — Loreto. 9km/5.6mi; 3h05min. Grade, equipment, access as main walk. Ask the taxi driver to take you to Rabaçal ('Rah-bah-**sahl**'). Follow the main walk from the Rabaçal houses (the 40min-point).

An awe-inspiring landscape, all stillness and solitude. The flanks of the Paúl da Serra stretch out before you, endlessly, under a porcelain-blue sky. Only your own shadow and a few sheep will walk with you on the 'marsh of the mountain range'.

The taxi will deposit you 9km up the road from Canhas, just before a small statue of Christ the King ('Cristo Rei'). Here the EN208 crosses the Levada do Paúl: there is a small waterhouse on the right and four concrete markers on the left. This is one of the island's older levadas, now integrated into the new scheme. Further east it is more accurately called the Levada da Bica da Cana, for it takes its source below Bica da Cana, in Ponta do Sol's river.

Begin the walk by striking out west (*P*32), looking down over the moors to the lush south coast. The landscape is reminiscent of the English moorlands, but with a difference: there is always the levada ribboning ahead of you — now silver, now amethyst, always mesmerising. There's a narrow bit of path by a waterfall in about five minutes, but no further obstacles. The vista stretching out before you seems to go on forever. At **25min** pass a river pool, fed by a waterfall; reach a second in **45min**. Here, caves stretch up on the right, into the hills (*P*32). Animals and shepherds shelter here in bad weather. In April the hillside is crowned with golden gorse; the levada mirrors the sky; a few baby goats dare to gambol along your path.

Cows graze freely here, on the lower slopes.

At **1h10min** an intrusion of the 20th century: you can see a metal conduit in the distance. It is carrying water from the reservoir above Rabaçal down to a power station. The turbines of this power station (commissioned 1953) feed on water from four separate levadas: you are walking one of them now, and Walk 33 shows you the other three. From the power station the water is sent eastwards to irrigate the fields of Calheta (14km/8.8mi of channels) and westwards to Ponta do Pargo (40km/25mi of channels). Walk 31 explores this levada, from Raposeira. At **1h15min** bear right on a track, just beyond a tiny chapel, to the main road (EN204). The levada continues through a short tunnel and then into a reservoir beside the road, from where it is piped down to the power station. There is an incredible feeling of *power* in the stillness.

Cross the EN204 and take the road to Rabaçal, rounding a U-turn and crossing the Ribeira do Alecrim with its lovely pools at **1h25min**. Continue downhill under the watchful eyes of goats until, at **1h40min**, you arrive at Rabaçal. While this rest house is usually reserved for the use of government employees, an overnight stay can sometimes be arranged (see 'Where to stay', page 36). When the tarred road ends at Rabaçal, turn right down the dirt track. In three minutes you come to the Risco levada. Follow the track beside it for five minutes, then fork left down a path, to the Levada das 25 Fontes. Turn left when you reach this levada (both of these levadas are explored at leisure in Walk 33). Fifteen minutes' walking along this enchanting, singing watercourse will bring you to a grassy sun-trap outside the entrance to the first major tunnel built

'There is always the levada, ribboning ahead of you' (Picnic 32).

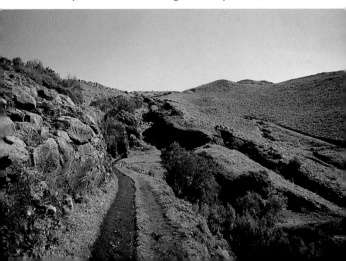

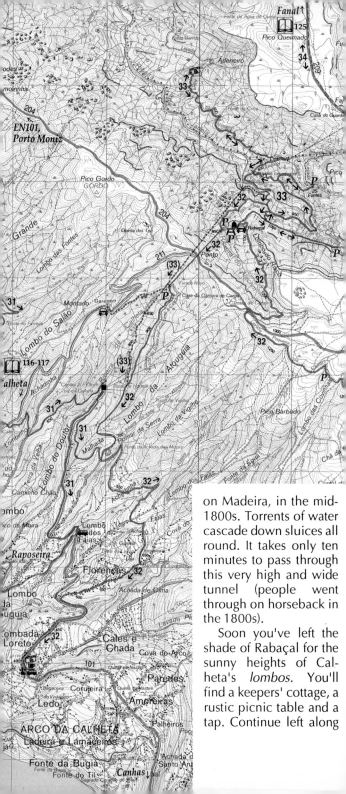

on Madeira, in the mid-1800s. Torrents of water cascade down sluices all round. It takes only ten minutes to pass through this very high and wide tunnel (people went through on horseback in the 1800s).

Soon you've left the shade of Rabaçal for the sunny heights of Calheta's *lombos*. You'll find a keepers' cottage, a rustic picnic table and a tap. Continue left along

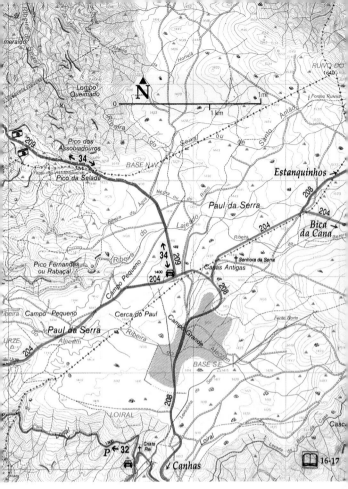

the levada *until you have crossed a small ravine with waterfalls via a bridge.* Then follow the adjacent path down the valley, through heath trees, mimosa and pine. In **2h40min** you will meet two pipes carrying water from the tank down to the power station. Five minutes later, a single pipe holds the flow of the levadas of Risco and 25 Fontes. Soon meet the Levada da Rocha Vermelha and follow its course to a small tank, whence it too shoots down to the power station.

From here a jeep track takes you to the wide Levada Calheta—Ponta do Pargo (**3h15min**). Turn left and enjoy a sunny stroll with splendid views over the south coast. Some thirty-five minutes along, turn right down any cobbled track to descend through scrumptious Florenças. Meet the main road at **4h15min**; turn left and find Loreto's plane-shaded centre and chapel after **4h45min**.

121

33 RABAÇAL'S LEVADAS

Map pages 120-121

Distance: 12.5km/7.8mi; 3h45min

Grade: moderate, with a **possibility of vertigo** on the levadas

Equipment: stout shoes (walking boots preferable), cardigans, long trousers, sunhat, anorak, whistle, rainhat, picnic, plastic bottle with water purifying tablets

How to get there and return: ⇌ (Car tours 5 and 6, but see also Alternative walk 1 below) or taxi to Rabaçal. Either hire a taxi for a full day, or first take a bus to 'Recta das Canhas' (see Walk 32, page 118).

Short walks

1 Rabaçal — Risco falls — Rabaçal. 1.7km/1mi; 30min. Easy. Access as above. Follow the main walk for 13min and return the same way.

2 Rabaçal — 25 Fontes — Rabaçal. 5km/3mi; 1h40min. Easy. Access as above. (Note: This route used to be very vertiginous, but wooden railings were built in 1992. Should they come down in storms, those prone to vertigo may have to turn back.) Follow the main walk for 5min and turn left down the path to the Levada das 25 Fontes. Follow the main walk from the 21min-point to 25 Fontes and return the same way.

Alternative walks

1 Rabaçal tunnel — Rabaçal levadas — Rabaçal tunnel. 16km/10mi; under 5h. Grade and equipment as main walk; take a torch as well. Access by ⇌. Some motorists may find the road to Rabaçal too hair-raising (Car tours 5 and 6). From the EN204 drive south on the EN211, and park about 2km downhill, by a derelict concrete building (now just a wall; 'Garagem' on the map). From there follow the dirt track northeast to the Rabaçal tunnel (*P*33c; 10min) and go through it (another 10min). You emerge at a sun-trap on the Levada das 25 Fontes (*P*33b). Follow the levada for 10 minutes, then turn right up a path to Rabaçal. Do the main walk in its entirety, but don't climb back up to Rabaçal; return to the sun-trap and through the tunnel, back to your car.

2 Rabaçal levadas — Rocha Vermelha tunnel — Loreto. 20.5km/ 12.7mi; about 6h. Grade: moderate, but sure-footedness and a head for heights essential. **Danger of vertigo** just before the tunnel. Equipment as above, plus torch. Access as main walk (taxi); return on ⇌ 80, 107, 139 or 150 from Loreto to Funchal. Do the entire main walk. At the 3h05min-point, instead of climbing up 185m/610ft to Rabaçal, continue through the Rocha Vermelha tunnel (20 minutes to pass), coming out in the Calheta Valley. Follow the levada to its 'tank' and there pick up the notes for Walk 32 (page 121), to continue to Loreto.

Rabaçal is an enchanted fairyland of singing waterfalls, a favourite excursion spot for the islanders. Here at the head of Madeira's greatest valley, the Rabaçal houses (*P*33a) lie dwarfed beneath emerald mountains. Three levadas draw their water here; each has its own 'person-ality', and this walk lets you make friends with all three.

The walk begins just where the tarred road ends at Rabaçal. Turn right down the dirt track. In **3min** you find yourself on the highest levada (1030m/3380ft), the Levada do Risco. Pass a fork to the Levada das 25 Fontes in **5min** and in **9min** ford a spillway created by a waterfall on

Vinte e Cinco Fontes ('25 Springs')

the right. Here the levada is flanked by an exceedingly beautiful mossy 'carpet'. (Levada works in the late 1980s necessitated the cutting of this track, and the old mossy way was destroyed, but it is so damp here that we are sure the levada will quickly regrow its mossy coat.) Notice that the banks of the watercourse are built up high to cope with a great flow. You reach Risco in **13min** (*P*33d). Here two falls cascade into a pool, from a height of 100m/325ft. The tunnel on your right was part of the works in the 1980s; they bored into the hillside to tap more underground springs for this levada. From here you can see the levada continue around the head of the gorge and along the valley opposite to its source in the Ribeira Grande. Look below, across the valley, to see a second channel cut into the mountainside: this is the 'middle' levada, leading to 25 Fontes ('25 Springs'). If you don't mind getting soaked, you can go under the waterfall to see Risco's pool, but beyond here the levada is completely crumbled away.

Now retrace your steps to the fork to 25 Fontes (**21min**). Bear right and climb down stone steps to reach the levada (altitude 960m/3150ft). Turn right and you will see the Risco waterfalls again, from a lower level: in **40min** you come to the head of the gorge where they dive down. Then cross the bed of the Ribeira Grande, to meet a tiny water-house: water is gushing out of its front door... After this point, the levada channel is only 30cm/1ft wide in places, and there are drops at the left of up to 30m/100ft. But even without railings we never found this levada vertiginous, because, unlike most others, it is built up off the path, not sunk into it. The concrete edge of the levada is at waist level, and you can hold on to it for moral support if the drops worry you. It's cooling to run your hands in the water on a hot day. In **1h** you pass the path down left to the Levada da Rocha Vermelha. Ignore it for the moment for, in about **1h10min** walking, in a tributary of the Cedros River, you reach a path leading up right (by a sluice), and at once you see a semi-circular bowl into which tumble down many sparkling waterfalls (but, alas, no longer 25). It's a lovely place to paddle under ferns (*P*33e).

From here return to the path passed ten minutes earlier. Turn down right (perhaps passing some beehives on your right). Try to keep on the main zigzag path; some of the short cuts are terribly steep. Soon you can see the levada below — the lowest of the Rabaçal levadas, at 850m/2790ft; you reach it in **1h35min**. A keepers' house sits below on your right. This levada is much wider than the other two and is the newest of the three. Turn right on it, back up into the valley of the Ribeira dos Cedros. There are waterfalls left, right and centre! Cross the Cedros on a concrete bridge and find a tunnel on your right: water is flowing in from mountains on the east side of the Seixal River, some 4km/2.5mi away. Turn left on the levada and follow it round the valley. Soon you're just opposite the *levadeiros'* house; some 215m/700ft directly above it you see the houses of Rabaçal. Notice how the levada narrows beyond each tributary, as you get nearer to the source. In **2h10min** you might like to take a break at a grassy promontory, from where there is a magnificent view of the Ribeira da Janela 200m/650ft below you.

Time constraints will limit the distance you can walk on this levada; we stop after **2h25min**, where the green line ends on the map. From here return the same way, enjoying grassy verges and the aroma of wild mint, open views and shady heath-tree bowers. You'll be back at the keepers' cottage in **2h55min**. Stay on the levada, passing the path where you came down to it, and turning up into the Ribeira Grande. The Risco falls and the 25 Fontes Levada are visible ahead and above you. Across this wild gulley yawns the Rocha Vermelha tunnel (Alternative walk 2); it disgorges in the Calheta Valley near the path of Walk 32. A bridge crosses the river, to the tunnel, but carry on past it, to the sluices and rock pools (**3h05min**), where you can take a break by the roaring (Risco) falls. Then cross the bridge and turn *sharp left* up a stone-laid path, to begin the climb to Rabaçal. In 20 minutes you reach the Levada das 25 Fontes, where you turn right. Ten minutes later, steps on the left take you up to Rabaçal (**3h45min**).

Map begins on page 120 and continues below; photograph page 128; STOP PRESS page 136.

Distance: 18km/11.2mi; 4h30min

Grade: easy, but danger of thick mists descending. (If this happens, do not stray off the track/road.)

Equipment: stout shoes (walking boots in wet conditions), sunhat, anorak, 2 cardigans, whistle, picnic, water

How to get there and return: 🚗 (Car tours 5 and 6) or taxi to the Paúl da Serra. Either hire a taxi for a full day, or first take a bus to 'Recta das Canhas' (see Walk 32, page 118) and arrange for the Canhas taxi driver to wait for you or to come back for you in time for your return bus. Ask the driver for 'Camino do Fanal' (Kah-**mee**-noh doh Fah-**nahl**).

Short walk: Paúl da Serra — Rabaçal/north coast overlook — Paúl da Serra. 4km/2.5mi; 1h. Grade, equipment, access as above.

The air will be crystal-clear, the panorama endless; and even with the sun fully up, dew-drops will sparkle on the gold-green grasses of the Paúl. You're bound for the Fanal, where ancient indigenous laurels are now under government protection. Hopefully only sea-gulls and butterflies will keep you company, not cars or jeeps.

The walk starts on the EN204, by the signpost 'Fanal/ Ribeira da Janela'. By **25min** you reach the deep valley of the Ribeira dos Cedros on the left (Walk 33 takes you up into this valley). Five minutes later, on your left, you overlook the red-tiled roofs of the Rabaçal houses and, just above them, the edge of the reservoir. To the right you can see the north coast; this is a delightful place to finish the Short walk with a picnic.

By about **1h50min** you are drawing near to a cone-shaped mound with trees parading up its left flank — Pedreira, landmark of the Fanal. Come to a track off right and follow it past the forestry house (**2h05min**). When you're well to the north of Pedreira, climb up the promontory at the right for lunch. From here you look down on the breathtaking beauty of Chão da Ribeira, the Ribeira do Seixal, and the sea.

Return the same way to your transport (**4h30min**).

35 LEVADA DA CENTRAL DA RIBEIRA DA JANELA

Distance: up to 9km/5.6mi; 2h30min

Grade: easy, but sure-footedness and a head for heights essential; **possibility of vertigo.**

Equipment: stout shoes (walking boots preferable), long trousers, cardigans, anorak, sunhat, rainhat, picnic, water, whistle

How to get there and return: 🚗 car or taxi to the reservoir above Porto Moniz. Ask a taxi driver for the 'Levada da Central, Lamaceiros' ('Lah-mah-**say**-roosh'). By car, drive uphill out of Porto Moniz: 3.5km up from the roundabout with a statue by the petrol station, turn left. Keep straight at any forks. Go through Lamaceiros (making sure you keep to the left of the church, 4.5km from the roundabout). At a very narrow U-turn (4.8km), go straight ahead on a dirt track for 100m and park: the levada is just ahead; its reservoir is to the left. If there is no room to park well off the track, go back 0.4km and park in Lamaceiros. *Note:* This walk is also accessible by 🚌 139 or 150 to Porto Moniz, then taxi as above. Walk 1.3km back to the EN101 at the Lamaceiros turn-off, for the return bus.

Short walk: See Picnic 35, page 15.

W e've not included many walks in the west of the island because access is so difficult. But Rodoeste has introduced an inexpensive 'see the island' circuit (bus 139), with a four-hour stop at Porto Moniz. Others of you,

In about 30 minutes the levada widens by a filtration point. The path is lined by fruit trees intertwined with passion flowers. This is an especially beautiful picnic spot (Picnic 35).

based at Porto Moniz, will probably have a car at your disposal. Why not take an hour or two to follow the levada that skirts the western flanks of the great Janela Valley? You will have stupendous views over the river and the terraces surrounding Ribeira da Janela.

Start out at the reservoir and follow the wide watercourse past huge bushes of fennel, apple and fig trees, and garlands of passion flowers. In **30min** the levada widens to canal-size, at a filtration point — a particularly lovely picnic setting (*P*35; see opposite). Five minutes later, notice the cables and pulleys used for hoisting supplies from the valley. Down along the river stretches one of the most impressive expanses of terracing on the island.

Within **45min** the sure-footed amongst you will reach a ferny glen in the upper reaches of the Ribeira da Cova. Soon you skirt a rock escarpment, where water pours down to feed the levada. In **1h** you are looking straight up the Janela Valley and, if you have binoculars, you'll easily see the Rabaçal houses (Walks 32 and 33).

The walk ends in **1h15min**, when you meet a tunnel in the Ribeira da Quebrada. (It takes 10 minutes to pass, but another tunnel lies beyond it, and the way becomes ever more vertiginous as the levada nears its source.) Turn back here, to catch the bus or return to your car (**2h30min**).

A country code for walkers and motorists

The experienced rambler is used to following a 'country code', but the tourist out for a lark may unwittingly cause damage, harm animals, and even endanger his own life. Please respect this country code.

- **Do not light fires.** Madeira's forests are her glory.
- **Do not damage levadas.** Don't touch sluice gates or the stones used to control small sluices.
- **Protect all wild and cultivated plants.** Don't pick wild flowers or saplings. ***Never cross cultivated land!***
- **Take all your litter away with you.**
- **Do not frighten animals.** They are *not tame.* By making loud noises, or trying to touch or photograph them, you may cause them to run in fear — over a precipice.
- **Leave all gates as you find them.** They have a purpose: generally to keep animals in — or out of — an area.
- **Walkers — DO NOT TAKE RISKS!** And remember:
  — **At any time a walk may become unsafe.** If the route is not as we describe it, if there is any sign of mist falling, or if it is late in the day, ***turn back!*** Remember, there is virtually *no twilight* on Madeira!
  — **Walks graded 'expert'** are usually unsuitable for winter walking.
  — **NEVER walk alone** — and **always** tell a responsible person *exactly* where you are going and what time you plan to return.
  — **Do not overestimate your capacity:** your speed will be determined by the slowest walker, and **bus connections** may be vital.
  — **Proper footwear is essential.**
  — **Mists can fall suddenly** on the Paúl da Serra and in the mountains.
  — **Warm clothing** and **extra rations** are needed in the mountains.
  — **Compass, whistle, torch, first-aid kit** weigh little, but might save your life. If you become lost or injure yourself, it may be a very long time before you are found, and there are *no* official rescue services.
  — **Protect yourself from the sun.**
  — **A stout stick** is a help on steep terrain and to discourage the rare unfriendly dog (see also note on page 38, 'Nuisances').
  — **Read and re-read the 'Important note'** on page 2 and guidelines on grade and equipment for each walk you plan to do.

The ancient laurels in the Fanal are now under government protection.

BUS TIMETABLES

Below is a list of destinations covered by these timetables. Numbers following place names are *bus numbers*; they are arranged below in numerical order. *But note that all orange 'town' buses are at the end of the list on page 133.* See page 9 for more bus information and pages 10-11 for bus departure points. **No buses run Christmas Day.**

Águas Mansas 60, 77
Assomada 2, 20, 23, 25, 53, 78, 113
Babosas *town* 22
Barreira *town* 11
Boa Morte 127, 148
Boaventura 6, 103
Boqueirão 60
Botanical Gardens *town* 29, 30
Cabo Girão 154
Calheta 80, 107, 139, 150
Camacha 29, 77
Campanário 4, 6, 7, 80, 107, 123, 139, 150
Candelária 80, 107
Canhas 80, 107, 139, 150
Caniçal 113
Caniço 2, 113, 155
Corticeiras 96
Cruz 53, 78
Cruzinhas 103
Curral das Freiras 81
Encumeada 6, 139, 150

Estreito de C.d. Lobos 3, 4, 6, 7, 80, 96, 107, 137, 139, 154
Faial 53, 78, 103
Fontes 127
Gaula 60
Ilha de São Jorge 103
Lombada *town* 1, 3
Lombo Grande 60
Loreto 80, 107, 139, 150
Machico 20, 23, 53, 78, 113, 156
Madalena do Mar 4
Maroços 156
Monte *town* 20, 21
Palheiro Ferreiro 29, 77, *town* 37
Pico do Facho 113
Poiso 103
Ponta da Oliveira 155
Ponta Delgada 6
Ponta do Pargo 80, 139, 150
Ponta do Sol 4, 107
Portela 20, 53, 78
Porto da Cruz 53, 78

Porto Moniz 80, 139, 150
Prazeres 80, 107, 139, 150
Raposeira 80, 107, 139, 150
Referta 53, 78
Ribeira Brava 4, 6, 7, 80, 107, 127, 139, 150
Ribeira de Machico 20, 53, 78
Ribeira Seca 113
Ribeiro Frio 103
Romeiros *town* 29
Santa Cruz 20, 23, 25, 53, 113, 156
Santa Quitéria *town* 8, 16
Santana 103
Santo da Serra 20, 25, 77, 78
São Vicente 6, 139, 150
Sitio Quatro Estradas 77
Stadium *town* 45
Trapiche *town* 11
Vinháticos 6, 139

2 Funchal • Assomada (journey time 40min)
Departs Funchal: 07.30, 08.30, 10.00, 11.00, 11.45*, 12.00•, 12.45*, 13.00•, 14.00*, 15.00, 16.00*, 16.30•, 17.00*, 17.45*, 18.00•, 18.45•, 19.00•, 19.30*, 20.15*, 20.30•, 21.00, 21.20#, 22.30, 23.45
Departs Assomada: 05.45, 06.20*, 06.45•, 07.00*, 07.40*, 08.10*, 08.30•, 09.30, 11.00, 11.40*, 12.00•, 12.25*, 13.30•, 13.45*, 14.45*, 15.00•, 16.00*, 17.00, 17.45, 18.30*, 19.00•, 19.30*, 20.20#, 21.30, 23.10

3 Funchal • Estreito de Câmara de Lobos (journey time 45min)
Departs Funchal: 07.45*#, 12.30*#, 14.05•, 16.00*#, 17.35□, 18.15*#, 19.15*#
Departs Estreito: 07.00*#, 07.30, 08.30, 09.00*#, 13.45*#, 15.15□•, 17.15*#

4 Funchal • Madalena do Mar (via Ribeira Brava and Ponta do Sol)
Funchal	10.05*	17.30‡	Madalena	05.50‡	12.40*
Ribeira Brava	11.30*	19.00‡	Ponta do Sol	06.00‡	12.55*
Ponta do Sol	12.00*	19.20‡	Ribeira Brava	06.25‡	13.25*
Madalena	12.10*	19.30‡	Funchal	07.40‡	14.40*

6 Funchal • Boaventura (via Ribeira Brava and São Vicente)
Funchal	07.35	13.35*	17.05★	Boaventura	05.50†	07.00★	14.40
Estreito C.d.L.	08.00	14.00*	17.30★	P. Delgada	06.00†	07.10★	14.50
Campanário	08.35	14.35*	18.00★	S. Vicente	06.20†	07.30★	15.10
Ribeira Brava	08.55	14.55*	18.20★	Encumeada	06.55†	08.05★	15.45
Vinháticos	09.30	15.30*	18.55★	Vinháticos	07.05†	08.15★	15.55
Encumeada	09.40	15.40*	19.05★	Ribeira Brava	07.40†	08.50★	16.30
São Vicente	10.15	16.15*	19.45★	Campanário	07.55†	09.05★	16.50
P. Delgada	10.35	16.35*	20.05★	Estreito C.d.L.	08.20†	09.30★	17.20
Boaventura	10.45	16.45*	20.15★	Funchal	08.45†	09.55★	17.45

*not Sundays or holidays; ‡ only Mon/Wed/Fri; •only Sundays/holidays; ★ not Good Friday, 26 or 31 Dec; † not Sundays or the first Saturday in Sept; # not Saturdays; □only Saturdays

7 Funchal • Ribeira Brava (journey time 1h30min)
Mondays to Fridays
Departs Funchal: 06.45, 09.30, 10.50, 14.00, 15.30, 17.00, 18.30■, 20.15
Departs Ribeira Brava: 06.05, 08.15, 11.00, 12.35, 15.30, 17.15, 18.35, 22.00
Sat/Sun/holidays
Departs Funchal: 06.45□, 10.05•, 10.50□, 12.05•, 13.30, 15.30, 17.00, 20.15
Departs Ribeira Brava: 06.05□, 08.15□, 11.00□, 11.45•, 12.30□, 13.35•, 15.30
17.05, 18.35

20 Funchal • Machico • Santo da Serra (via Portela)

Funchal	07.15*	12.40	16.30*	19.15+	20.45+
Machico	08.10*	13.35	17.25*	20.10+	21.40+
Santo da Serra (arrives)	08.55*	14.20	18.10*	20.55+	—
Santo da Serra (departs)	06.30*	08.00*	09.45*	10.00•	14.45+
Machico	07.15*	08.45*	10.30*	10.45•	15.30+
Funchal	08.10*	09.40*	11.25*	—	16.25+

Passes Portela about 10min before arriving/after departing Santo da Serra

23 Funchal • Machico (via Santa Cruz; journey time 55min)
Departs Funchal: 08.00□, 08.30□, 10.30*, 13.30•, 13.45•, 15.45•, 21.00•, 21.30
Departs Machico: 05.30*, 06.30*, 07.30*, 09.30•, 11.45*, 12.45*, 18.30•, 20.00□,
21.15+, 22.45+

25 Funchal • Santo da Serra (via Santa Cruz; journey time 1h15min)
Departs Funchal: 08.45•
Departs Santo da Serra: 16.15• (1.10-31.5) or 17.45• (1.6-30.9)

29 Funchal • Camacha (journey time 40min)
weekdays
Departs Funchal: 08.00, 09.00, 10.00, 11.00, 11.45, 13.00#, 15.30, 16.30#,
17.00#, 17.30, 18.00#, 18.30#, 19.00, 19.30#, 20.00#, 20.30
Departs Camacha: 07.00, 07.15#, 07.45#, 08.15, 08.45, 09.45, 10.45, 11.45,
14.15, 15.30#, 16.15, 17.15#, 17.45#, 18.15, 18.45#, 19.15#, 19.45, 22.45#
Sundays/holidays
Departs Funchal: 09.15, 10.00, 11.00, 12.30, 15.30, 17.00, 19.00, 20.45
Departs Camacha: 08.30, 10.00, 11.00, 11.45, 14.45, 16.15, 17.45, 20.15

53 Funchal • Machico • Ribeira de Machico • Portela • Porto da Cruz • Faial

Funchal	—	10.00*	13.00*	—	17.20*	18.15•	19.15+
Machico	08.30¶	10.50*	13.50•	14.30•	18.10•	19.05•	20.05+
Portela	09.05¶	11.25*	14.25*	15.05•	18.45*	19.35•	20.40+
P. da Cruz	09.20¶	11.40*	14.40*	15.20•	19.00*	19.50•	20.55+
Faial (arr)	09.30¶	12.00*	15.00*	15.30•	19.15*	20.00•	21.15+
Faial (dep)	05.45+	10.00	13.00•	15.30*	16.45*		
P. da Cruz	05.55+	10.10	13.10•	15.40*	16.55*		
Portela	06.10+	10.25	13.25•	15.55*	17.10*		
Machico	06.45+	11.00	14.00•	16.30*	17.45*		
Funchal	07.35+	11.50	—	17.20*	18.35*		

60 Funchal • Boqueirão (via Gaula; journey time 1h)
Departs Funchal: 11.00, 13.30+, 17.00+, 18.30§, 19.15+
buses pass Gaula approx. 10min and Lombo Grande 5min before Boqueirão
Departs Boqueirão: 06.15*, 06.30•, 07.30*, 08.30*, 12.30*, 16.00•, 16.30*
buses pass Lombo Grande approx. 5min and Gaula 10min after Boqueirão

77 Funchal • Santo da Serra (via Camacha)

Funchal	07.35*	08.30•	10.30	14.00	16.00	18.00*	19.15
Camacha	08.10*	09.10•	11.10	14.40	16.40	18.40*	19.55
Sitio Quatro Estradas	08.40*	09.40•	11.40	15.10	17.10	19.10*	20.25
Santo da Serra (arrives)	08.50*	09.50•	11.50	15.20	17.20	19.20*	20.35

+ Mon-Fri; ■not on 31 Dec or 1 Jan; □ only Saturdays; *not Sundays or holidays; ‡only Mon/
Wed/Fri; •only Sundays/holidays; † not Sundays or the first Saturday in Sept; #not Saturdays;
§ Sat/Sun/holidays only; ¶ in the school season only

77 Funchal • Santo da Serra (via Camacha) *continued*

Santo da Serra (dep)	09.15*	10.00•	12.00#	16.15*	18.00•	20.40*#
Sítio Quatro Estradas	09.20*	10.00•	12.05#	16.20*	18.05•	20.45*#
Camacha	09.55•	10.40•	12.40#	16.55*	18.40•	21.20*#
Funchal	10.35•	11.20•	13.20#	17.35*	19.20•	22.00*#

78 Funchal • Machico • Faial (via Santo da Serra, Portela, Porto da Cruz)

Funchal	08.00•	12.30**	16.15*		Faial	06.45**	17.30•
Machico	08.50•	13.20**	17.05*		Machico	07.45**	18.40•
Faial (arrives)	10.00•	14.30**	18.30*		Funchal (arrive)	08.35**	19.40•

From Machico add approx. 30min to Portela, 40min to Santo da Serra; 1h to Porto da Cruz
From Faial add approx.10min to Porto da Cruz, 20min to Portela, 30min to Santo da Serra

80 Funchal to Porto Moniz (via Calheta)

Funchal (departs*) 14.35; Ribeira Brava 16.00; Calheta 17.10; Raposeira 17.55;
Ponta do Pargo 18.15; Porto Moniz (arrives) 19.00
Porto Moniz (departs */*) 16.00; Ponta do Pargo 16.35; Raposeira 17.05; Calheta
17.35; Ribeira Brava 18.50; Funchal (arrives) 20.00

81 Funchal • Curral das Freiras (journey time 1h15min)

Departs Funchal: 05.15*, 07.45#, 11.00, 13.15+, 16.30, 19.30*
Departs Curral: 06.45*, 08.45#, 12.15, 14.30+, 17.15, 20.30*

96 Funchal • Corticeiras (via Estreito de Câmara de Lobos; journey time 1h)

Mondays to Fridays
Departs Funchal: 07.00, 07.40, 08.05, 09.05, 09.45, 10.45, 11.45, 12.15, 13.15,
14.15, 15.15, 16.15, 16.45, 17.30, 18.15, 18.30, 18.45, 19.15, 19.50, 21.05
Departs Corticeiras: 05.00, 06.00, 06.30, 06.45, 08.05, 08.45, 09.05, 10.15,
11.00, 12.00, 12.45, 13.30, 14.30, 15.15, 16.15, 17.15, 18.00, 19.00, 20.00
Saturdays, Sundays and holidays
Departs Funchal: 07.05, 08.05, 09.15, 11.15, 12.05□, 13.00, 15.00, 16.00, 17.30
Departs Corticeiras: 08.05, 09.05, 10.15, 11.00, 12.45, 13.05□, 14.50, 16.05,
17.05, 18.35, 20.00
Arrives Estreito 45min after departing Funchal and 15min after departing Corticeiras

103 Funchal • Boaventura (via Faial)

Funchal	07.30	13.30◇	16.00•	18.00•
Poiso	08.30	14.30◇	17.00•	19.00•
Ribeiro Frio	08.40	14.40◇	17.10•	19.10•
Cruzinhas	09.00	15.00◇	17.30•	19.30•
Faial	09.15	15.15◇	17.45•	19.45•
Santana	09.45	15.45◇	18.15•	20.15•
São Jorge (and Ilha)	10.15	16.15◇	18.45•	20.45•
Boaventura (arrives)	11.15	17.15◇	19.45•	21.45•
Boaventura (departs)	05.30◇	07.15	12.00•	16.00
São Jorge (and Ilha)	06.30◇	08.15	13.00•	17.00
Santana	07.00◇	08.45	13.30•	17.30
Faial	07.30◇	09.15	14.00•	18.00
Cruzinhas	07.45◇	09.30	14.15•	18.15
Ribeiro Frio	08.05◇	09.50	14.35•	18.35
Poiso	08.15◇	10.00	14.45•	18.45
Funchal	09.00◇	11.00	15.45•	19.45

107 Funchal • Raposiera

Funchal	08.05	16.05+✤	Raposeira	07.10+✤	15.35
Ribeira Brava	09.30	17.30+✤	Prazeres	07.20+✤	15.45
Canhas	10.10	18.10+✤	Calheta (Estrela ✈)	07.35+✤	16.00
Calheta (Estrela ✈)	10.45	18.45+✤	Canhas	08.10+✤	16.35
Prazeres	11.00	19.00+✤	Ribeira Brava	08.35+✤	17.00
Raposiera	11.10	19.10+✤	Funchal	10.00+✤	18.15

* only Saturdays; * not Sundays or holidays; • only Sundays/holidays; # not Saturdays; ✤ except
6 Jan, 25, 26 Dec, via the coastal road and Ponta do Sol; ** holidays only; */* not Tuesdays or
Wednesdays; ◇ not on Sundays or on 1 Jan, Good Friday, 15 Aug, 26 Dec; + not on 14 Aug

113 Funchal • Caniçal (via Santa Cruz and Machico; journey time 1h15min)
Departs Funchal (for Machico): 07.30, 08.30+, 09.00, 11.15*, 12.15, 14.30*, 15.00•, 15.30*, 16.30•, 17.15*, 18.15+, 19.00•, 19.30•, 19.45▫, 22.30+
Departs Machico (for Caniçal): 08.25, 09.25+, 09.55, 12.10*, 13.10, 15.25*, 15.55•, 16.25*, 17.25•, 18.10*, 19.10*, 19.55•, 20.25+, 20.40▫, 23.25
Departs Caniçal (for Machico): 05.45*, 06.45, 07.30+, 09.30, 10.30*, 11.55, 13.10*, 14.10, 17.10, 18.10*, 19.10•, 19.40*, 21.00•
Departs Machico (for Funchal): 06.05*, 07.05, 07.50+, 09.50, 10.50*, 12.15, 13.30*, 14.30, 17.30, 18.30*, 19.30•, 20.00*, 21.20•

123 Funchal • Campanário (journey time 1h05min)
Departs Funchal 13.00+, 18.05#, 19.05*; Departs Campanário: 14.15+

127 Ribeira Brava • Boa Morte (journey 25min) • Fontes (journey 55min)
Departs Ribeira Brava: 07.45★ (only Mondays, Wednesdays), 08.45★ (not Mondays, Wednesdays), 11.10★, 13.15★
Buses underlined end at Boa Morte; no suitable departures from Fontes or Boa Morte

137 Funchal • Estreito de Câmara de Lobos (journey time 55min)
Departs Funchal: 08.00, 10.30, 12.20, 14.15*, 16.25, 17.15+, 18.15, 19.15*
Departs Estreito: 08.15, 09.15, 11.25, 13.15, 15.10*, 17.15, 19.10*

139 Funchal • Porto Moniz • Funchal (not Tuesdays or Wednesdays)
Funchal (depart)	09.00	Porto Moniz (depart)	16.00
Ribeira Brava	10.25	Calheta	17.35
São Vicente	11.30	Ribeira Brava	18.50
Porto Moniz (arrive)	12.15	Funchal (arrive)	20.00

148 Funchal • Boa Morte (journey time 1h25min)
Departs Funchal: 13.05★*, 18.05★*; Departs Boa Morte: 14.30★*

150 Funchal • Porto Moniz (via São Vicente)
Funchal (dep)	09.00	17.35	Porto Moniz (dep)	05.20
Ribeira Brava	10.15	18.45	Seixal	05.40
São Vicente	11.30	20.00	São Vicente	06.00
Seixal	11.40	20.15	Ribeira Brava	07.15
Porto Moniz (arr)	12.15	20.55	Funchal (arr)	08.30

NB: *The 09.00 bus runs daily, **except Tuesdays and Wednesdays**, to Porto Moniz. It leaves Porto Moniz at **about** 16.00 (**verify!**) and returns to Funchal along the same route as bus 139.*

154 Funchal • Cabo Girão (journey time 1h)
Departs Funchal: 09.15+, 12.00+, 17.00+; Departs Cabo Girão: 13.15+, 18.00+
On Saturdays, Sundays, holidays, only one departure: Funchal 10.35; Cabo Girão 11.50

155 Funchal • Ponta da Oliveira (via Garajau or **via Figueirinhas)
Mondays to Saturdays
Departs Funchal: 06.30, 08.20, 10.15, 12.30, 13.30**, 14.15, 15.30#, 17.15**, 18.00, 19.15
Departs Ponta da Oliveira: 07.05, 09.00**, 11.00, 13.10, 14.15**, 15.00, 16.15#, 18.15**, 18.45, 20.00
Sundays and holidays
Departs Funchal: 08.15, 13.30**, 17.15**
Departs Ponta da Oliveira: 07.15, 09.00**, 14.15**, 18.15**

156 Funchal • Machico (journey time 55min) • Maroços (journey 1h15min)
Departs Funchal: 06.45*, 08.00+, 10.30•, 11.45, 13.15+, 13.45▫, 16.00*, 17.30+, 17.45, 19.00*, 20.00+, 20.30▫, 21.30•, 23.45
Departs Maroços: 05.45, 06.15*, 07.30*, 08.15, 09.45+, 11.30•, 13.00•, 13.30+, 15.30*, 15.45•, 20.00•, 22.30•
Departs Machico 55min after departing Funchal and 20min after departing Maroços

▫ only Saturdays; *not Sundays or holidays; •only Sundays/holidays; ★not Good Friday, 25, 26, 31 Dec, 1 Jan; # not Saturdays; +Mon-Fri only

HORARIOS DO FUNCHAL (orange town buses)

4 Funchal • Lombada ('Ponta da Laranjeira' bus; journey time approx. 30min)
Services too numerous to list; generally half-hourly (hourly on Sundays)

3 Funchal • Lombada (journey time approx. 30min)
Services too numerous to list; generally every 20 minutes (hourly on Sundays)

5 Funchal • Lido (journey time approx. 20min)
Buses leave Funchal at 20 and 50min past the hour daily, from 07.50 to 18.50
Buses leave the Lido at 05 and 35min past the hour daily, from 08.05 to 19.05

8 Funchal • Santa Quitéria (journey time approx. 30min)
Services too numerous to list; buses operate at least hourly, including Sundays

11 Funchal • Trapiche/Barreira (journey time approx. 30min)
Services too numerous to list; buses operate at least hourly, including Sundays

16 Funchal • Santa Quitéria (journey time approx. 30min)
Departs Funchal: 07.55, 08.10, 08.40, 10.00, 12.45, 13.15, 15.00 (Mon-Fri);
08.10, 10.00, 15.00 (Sat); no Sunday service
Departs Santa Quitéria: 13.15, 13.45, 15.30, 18.50, 19.20, 19.45, 20.15 (Mon-Fri);10.30, 15.35, 17.35 (Sat); no Sunday service

20 and 21 Funchal • Monte (journey time approx. 30min)
Services too numerous to list; buses operate at least half-hourly

22 Funchal • Babosas (journey time approx. 30min)
Services too numerous to list; generally hourly every day of the week. In 'rush hours' service is half-hourly

29 Funchal • Romeiros (via Jardim Botânico; journey time approx. 30min)
Departs Funchal: 07.00*, 07.45, 08.15+, 08.45, 11.00, 12.05+, 12.30, 13.00, 13.30, 15.30, 17.30, 18.30
Departs Romeiros: 08.15, 9.30, 11.30, 13.00, 13.30, 14.00, 16.00, 18.00, 19.00, 20.00, 21.00

30 Funchal • Jardim Botânico (journey time approx. 15min)
Departs Funchal: 07.30, 08.00*, 08.25, 09.25, 10.00*, 10.25, 11.30, 12.00§, 14.00, 16.00§, 16.30, 17.00, 18.00, 19.15+, 21.30
Departs Jardim Botânico: 08.00, 08.30*, 09.00, 10.00, 10.35*, 11.05, 12.00, 12.35§, 14.30, 15.05, 16.35§, 17.00, 17.35, 18.30§, 19.40+, 22.05

37 Funchal • Palheiro Ferreiro (journey time approx. 25min)
Departs Funchal 07.45+, 08.15•, 12.00+, 13.15, 17.15+, 18.25•
Departs Palheiro Ferreiro: 08.20+, 08.50•, 12.35+, 13.50, 17.55+, 18.20+, 19.00#

45 Funchal • Stadium ('Nazaré' bus; journey time approx. 10min)
Services too numerous to list; buses operate at least hourly every day of the week, half-hourly during 'rush-hours' Mondays to Fridays

NB: If you plan to make good use of the town buses, a weekly tourist pass (available at any of the circular green kiosks on the Avenida do Mar) is very good value. (To obtain one, you must have your passport with you.) Otherwise, pay the driver as you board. The same fare applies to *all* destinations: find out the current price and keep small notes handy; there are no conductors to give change, and the buses are very busy.

§ Sat/Sun/holidays only; +Mon-Fri; # not Saturdays; *not Sundays or holidays

Index

Geographical entries only are included here; for other entries, see Contents, page 3. A page number in **bold type** indicates a photograph; a page number in *italics* refers to a map (*TM* refers to the large scale walking map on the reverse of the touring map). For pronunciation hints, see page 136. For buses, see Timetables index, page 129.

134

Pronunciation/translation of some index entries

achada (ah-sháh-dah) small plateau

água (áh-gwah) water

arco (áhr-koh) arc or curving mountain ridge

baía (bah-ée-ah) bay

balcões (bahl-kóyngs) balconies

baixo (bíe-joh) lower

bica (bée-kah) small spring

boca (bóh-kah) mountain pass (literally 'mouth')

brava (bráh-vah) wild

cabo (káh-boh) cape

caldeirão (kahl-day-roúngh) cauldron, crater, basin

calheta (kahl-yáy-tah) creek

câmara (káh-mah-rah) chamber

camino (kah-mée-noh) way, path, road

campo (káhm-poh) plain

caniço (kah-née-soh) reed

chão (shoúng) flat place

choupana (show-páh-nah) cottage

corticeiras (kohr-tee-sáy-rahs) small cork trees

cova (kóh-vah) pit, cave

cruz (krúj) cross

cruzinhas (kru-zéen-yahs) crossroads

curral (koo-ráhl) corral

dentro (déhn-troh) inside

eira (éye-rah) threshing floor

encumeada (in-koo-mee-áh-dah) summit with fine views

estanquinhos (esh-tahn-kéen-ohs) small ponds

estreito (esh-tráy-toh) the straits above

faial (fye-áhl) beech grove

fajã (fah-jáh) small landslip

fonte (fóhn-tay) spring

fora (fór-ah) outside

janela (jha-náy-lah) window

jardim (jahr-déengh) garden

lamaceiros (lah-mah-sáy-roosh) marshy place

lapa (láh-pah) cave, den

levada (leh-váh-dah) watercourse (see page 6)

lombada (lohm-báh-dah) long ridge

lombo (lóh-moh) ridge separating two parallel ravines

miradouro (mee-rah-dó-roh) viewpoint

monte (móhn-teh) mount

mouro (móor-oh) Moor

nogueira (noh-gáy-rah) nut tree

palheiro (pahl-yáh-roh) cow house, thatched cottage

paragem (par-ráh-jengh) bus stop

paúl (pah-óol) marshland

penha (péyn-yah) rocky hill or cliff

pico (pée-koh) peak

poio (póy-oh) terrace

poiso (póy-soh) pause

ponta (póhn-tah) point

portela (pohr-táy-lah) little gateway

porto (póhr-toh) port

prazer (pra-zéhr) pleasure

quebrada (kay-bráh-dah) steep slope

queimada (kay-máh-dah) burnt

rabaça (rah-báh-sah) wild celery

recta (ráy-tah) straight (often a straight stretch of road)

ribeira (ree-báy-rah) river or river valley

risco (réesh-koh) danger

rocha (róh-shah) rock, crag

seixal (sáy-shal) pebbly place

serra (séh-rah) mountain range

sitio (sée-tee-oh) place

torre (tóh-ray) tower

torrinhas (toh-réen-yahs) turrets

vale (váh-l) vale, valley

vinhático (veen-yáh-tee-koh) indigenous laurel

STOP PRESS ▬▬▬▬▬▬

Car tours: The Funchal ring road is open to just west of Câmara de Lobos.

Walk 1 and Picnic 1: There is a new bridge crossing the ring road between Lombada and the levada.

Walk 2: The initial 100m/yds from the Sta. Quitéria bus stop is *uphill* now; after that the route descends as described. The levada channel between São Martinho and Curral was repaired and could be followed by **expert sure-footed walkers** in winter 1994. But in May 1994 a landslide destroyed the levada channel at Fajã and the path to Fajã. We expect the damage to the levada to be quickly repaired, but we are not certain whether the path to Fajã will be cleared.

Walk 3: A new road now extends up to the school at Curral de Baixo. Catch the bus at the bridge over the river (*paragem* sign).

Walk 4: Plans for a road into the Poço Valley seem to be abandoned at present.

Walk 7, Short walk 1: The levada starts just behind the school. **Short walk 2:** The road to Ribeirinha is tarred. **Short walks 3 and 4** are extremely vertiginous in places.

Walk 8: The cobbled track at the start of the walk is tarred as far as the school.

Walk 10, Short walk 3 is 6km/3.7mi; 1h40min, *not* 12km; 3h15min.

Walk 11 and Picnic 11: The old mill at the 5min-point has been rebuilt. Roadworks (to Ribeira de Machico) currently end at Maroços, where the 156 bus terminates.

Walk 17: A No 91 bus runs hourly from Barreira to Trapiche; change at Trapiche for the No 11 bus to Funchal.

Walk 21: Unreliable heath-tree branches now edge the large water tank by the Pico Ruivo tunnel.

Walk 23: Roadworks may interrupt this walk east of Torrinhas. Before setting out for Encumeada, enquire at the Pico Ruivo rest house if the route is passable.

Walk 24: Expect roadworks anywhere along the route. A new road is being built from Cruzinhas to Faial. It is unclear at time of writing whether it will destroy the old trail entirely. At present, the trail is being preserved, just beside the new road.

Walk 27: You will be confronted by a sign forbidding entry, just below the peak. We think this can be safely ignored; the peak is not private property.

Walk 29: The levada is now easily accessible. Follow the EN204 to the Bica da Cana signpost (1h15min). After a couple of minutes, at a promontory on the left-hand side of the road, scramble down to the levada just a few metres/yards below the road. Follow it down past the refurbished house.

Walk 31: If you walk west from Calheta, start from the EN211 just west of the power station; the levada is too vertiginous to follow between this road and the power station.

Walk 33: The bridge across the Cedros (1h35min) was broken and impassable for vertigo sufferers in summer 1994.

Walk 34: It appears that plans are going ahead to tar the road to Ribeira da Janela. It's very unlikely to see much traffic. If it *is* tarred by the time you use this book, do be sure to drive to Fanal, if you don't like walking on asphalt